ANTidote

David Winship

Copyright © 2016 David Winship

All rights reserved.

ISBN: 1530860725
ISBN-13: 978-1530860722

FOR LISA

All you need is hartglue – medicine for the soul.

Contents

GRANDMA'S STORY 8

HEY CAN I HAVE MY HAT BACK PLEASE? 17

THIS WAY UP 33

MARY POPPINS 47

BLOOD MOON RISING 55

APORIA 68

BITTER FRUIT 81

FISH OUT OF WATER 98

THIS LOVE-STARVED HEART OF MINE 112

LAMBDA 121

NEVER EXPLAIN ANYTHING 144

LEARNING FROM GEESE 153

NO BIG DEAL 166

THE FOOTBRIDGE 177

BIG LEAP OF FAITH 187

GRANDMA'S STORY

The moral of this story is: choose your grandmother very carefully. Yes I know that part is supposed to come at the end, but I must insure against the possibility that you won't reach it! So, anyway…

On my fourth birthday, my dad gave me a pink helium filled balloon dog (I wanted a real puppy, but hey) and I released it into the sky. Obviously it will have burst or something at a certain altitude. But I didn't know that at the time. I assumed it would float off into space and land on a remote planet where it would be discovered by a little alien boy or girl. I remember hoping he or she would appreciate the gesture and send the dog back after a day or two. We'd be like intergalactic balloon buddies.

Preposterous, obviously. And yet, here I am, a grown man in his forties, fronting a project to communicate with extraterrestrials. Well? What do you want me to say? I guess I still want my dog back.

I started RECONNECT in 2090. It isn't a research service agency as such. Nor is it a quango. Strictly speaking, it's not a World Security Council department or institute. It's been evolving in a kind of surreal twilight world of rose-coloured telescopes, dependent on global taxpayer funding (but without any real scrutiny on behalf of the taxpayer). Actually, to tell the truth, because the venture capital invested in it is allocated at the whim and discretion of a small circle of WSC senior representatives, it's funded without the taxpayer knowing *anything* about it. Seriously. I'm not joking. But hey, that has been pretty much standard procedure within the research sector in the 2080s and 2090s.

When my dad first told me my grandmother's story shortly after her death in 2078, I didn't believe a word of it. Not a single word. Not until I happened to do a bit of research (for Apeiron) into the Nebraska flying ant swarms of 2047, the year I was born. As I'm sure you're aware, the phenomenon was eventually linked with the Formica virus, blamed for a bizarre condition characterised by involuntary exclamations of Latin words and phrases. The World Health Organisation had declared it a Public Health Emergency of International Concern. Eventually, of course, the outbreak was controlled by deploying genetically modified ants, armed with an offspring-killing gene, to breed with the invading species.

Anyway, long story short, I was persuaded in the course of my investigations that this invasion by billions of mysterious bugs, turning the sky black for almost an entire month, may well have been a failed attempt at a planetary coup by tiny creatures from another world. In the end, I started to heed my dad's insistence that they had been chilloks from the planet Oov, so meticulously described by my grandmother in her account of her Morys Minor encounters.

To say my first attempts to get to the bottom of Grandma's story were tentative is to understate the case to the nth degree - I'd say about as tentative as a hatchling sea turtle trying to make the perilous journey to the water's edge before being picked off by predators. Uh huh. And there are donkey rides in the area. Oh, yes, and there's broken glass and some plastic can holders. Did I mention the tractor-towed beach cleaner? Anyway, obviously, I hadn't expected anyone to take my project seriously, and I was just astonished when first Apeiron, then the World Intelligence Agency and then the WSC itself, offered support, funding and accreditation. Gobsmacked. Okay, Grandma's narrative may have been detailed and expansive, but to give you some idea of just how implausible it must have sounded, the following is an unedited extract from my initial submission to the WSC's research accreditation unit:

"The Voyager 1 space probe was launched by NASA on September 5, 1977, to study the outer solar system and, ultimately, interstellar space. It carried a gold-plated audio-visual disc in the event that it might be found by intelligent life-forms from other planetary systems. The record contained photos of the Earth and its life-forms, spoken greetings from people including the President of the United States (Jimmy Carter), and a medley of sounds from Earth, including whales, a baby crying, waves breaking on a shore and music, including Chuck Berry's 'Johnny B. Goode' and works by Mozart. It was discovered by goopmutt bandits who towed it through interstellar space at superluminal speed. In an effort to conceal their crime, they manipulated the data on the craft's digital tape recorder and left it in the heliosphere where its signal could still be picked up from Earth.

Eventually, they abandoned the probe in the Centaurus galaxy where it was picked up by two itinerant spacecombers from a small circumbinary planet known as Morys Minor.

The discovery of the golden record attached to the Voyager probe raised expectations of harmonious relations between inhabitants of the two planets. To that end, one of the spacecombers who discovered it, smolin9, was dispatched by wormhole to Earth to investigate the planet and determine its suitability for colonisation. However, after extensive study and curious encounters with significant people including Barack Obama, the Mortians decided the planet exceeded volatility thresholds and deemed it unsuitable. One consequence of smolin9's time spent on Earth was his marriage to my grandmother, Melinda Hill of Camden in London..."

You with me so far? Okay, cool. I'll continue. No wait, I'll just take this opportunity to tell you my grandmother's advice for anyone considering marrying an extraterrestrial – go ahead and do it if you've got nothing better to do and you find conversations about the weather boring and you enjoy travel. Uh huh, yep, that's it. Sorry.

"...smolin9 eventually persuaded my grandmother to travel by wormhole to Morys Minor where she

was obliged to undergo various medical procedures designed to facilitate her survival on the planet, the most significant of which was an operation on her heart. Initially unaware of the implications, she was distraught to discover that the modification to her heart tissue was irreversible. It meant she could only return to Earth if a Mortian heart donor could be found (Mortian hearts function perfectly on both Morys Minor and Earth). Curiously, the situation resolved itself when a bizarre set of misunderstandings led to smolin9's associate, polkingbeal67, swapping hearts with her…"

Okay, I've got a sense that your eyes are starting to glaze over. In order that future generations will know the truth, I really *should* provide you with the *full* text from my submission, but I don't want to lose you. I'll paraphrase the rest of it.

For some curious reason, the Mortian leader decided to appoint my grandmother as his successor. Polkingbeal67, bristling with rage at losing his Mortian heart, set off for Heaven. He had persuaded himself that Heaven was actually a satellite of the Earth. Somehow, however, he managed to get his spacecraft hopelessly ensnared in space jelly in the vicinity of the Ring Nebula. A young cadet known as yukawa3 was dispatched to rescue him. An unpredictable and harrowing series of events led to the tragic death of smolin9. My grandmother, overcome with grief, decided to rename the planet 'Smolin9' in loving memory of her Mortian husband.

I often wonder if the commissioners actually got this far when they read my submission. But I suppose they might have done – after all, *you* have!

Anyway, my grandmother thwarted an attempted subjugation of her adopted planet by chilloks and, as an outlandish consequence of this, NASA's Voyager 1 space probe ended up being teleported from the Mortian leader's garden to the very doorstep of the President of the United States. Attached to the outside of the probe, in place of the golden record, was one of yukawa3's yellow sou'westers.

Listen, I appreciate that I'm asking you to believe some seriously weird stuff here. Stuff that flies in the face of reason like a wasp that won't go away and leave you alone. But I have a serious story to tell here – one that may, if you let it, sting you into a radically new understanding of the human condition and our place in the cosmos. I'm truly sorry if you were thinking you just wanted to chill out for a while with an ice-cool beer and a bit of mindless escapism. But I'm afraid these apparently bizarre details are important. Collecting them now may seem like trying to pick up a puddle of ice-cool beer, and that puddle may have a wasp floating in it, but I promise, yes, I promise you will be glad of all this later. Anyway, I've nearly finished.

After a great deal of soul-searching, my grandmother resolved to return to Earth, leaving polkingbeal67 as the rightful heir to power on Smolin9. A ceremony was held, marking both my grandmother's departure and polkingbeal67's confirmation as leader-elect. The incredible connection between Smolin9 and our own planet was sundered.

Totally plausible, right? Well, the WSC clearly thought so, because they not only agreed to support my application for a modestly-sized radio telescope, but they went *way* further than that and commissioned the CONNECT subterranean observatory in Nuneaton for the purpose of "intercepting alien wormhole communications by tracking quasinormal resonance and reflection/transmission coefficients." What? I know! I don't understand it either!

They insisted on calling the observatory CONNECT rather than RECONNECT. I think that's because they were happy with the idea of contact with alien civilisations so long as there was no risk of them having to reveal to the world that such contact had already taken place and that extraterrestrial beings had already enjoyed cosy little chats with people like Barack Obama and the Queen of England. Apparently, it's easier to justify spending money on phone calls to ET if the public thinks ET doesn't exist!

I'll never fully understand it, but the WSC were eating from my hand. Obviously I wasn't taking anything for granted, not least because the last time I had anyone eating out of my hand, I got bitten by a rabbit. By the way, did I mention they agreed to an initial capital outlay of WD30 billion? Yay! The only thing I had to fork out for was the paltry administration fee of three world dollars I had to send with the submission.

But, hey, I'll absorb the three dollars because, you know, that's just the kind of guy I am.

HEY CAN I HAVE MY HAT BACK PLEASE?

Another day, another conference and, once again, WSC delegates are spitting venom at each other as they stalk the mahogany Art Deco corridors of the vast underground CONNECT observatory in Nuneaton. Actually, the spitting venom thing is being conducted through the media, since the delegates refuse to sit together in the same room.

The same thing happened two weeks ago, to no discernible effect apart for an intensification of hostilities. Why should it be any different now? But it could and should have been so different. When the ETI signal was first detected, the mood had been euphoric, even if some of the executives had been utterly bewildered by yukawa3's clear, unambiguous neutrino message - "Hey, can I have my hat back, please?"

Anyway, arguments about how to proceed have raged and raged like a, um, raging animal thing. Should we go public with the news? Or should we keep schtum? I mean, who cares? Surely, what we *should* be worrying about is how to respond? Well, round here, the only people sitting on the fence are the astronomers and the scientists, but they're outnumbered by the managers and executives by a ratio of about forty to one. Of course, I know what will happen. Eventually, the debate will become hopelessly polarised and both camps will dig themselves into holes like armadillos. Stalemate will become the order of the day until someone loses patience and decides to pull them out by their tails one more time. Typically, that someone is me.

"What exactly is all this stuff about the 'at anyway?" Aysha asks.

I start to explain about yukawa3's penchant for collecting sou'westers and the significance of the one attached to the Voyager probe, so sensationally discovered on the White House lawn decades ago, but Aysha bares her perfect teeth and delivers a playful slap to my chest with the back of her hand. "We-e-ell," she growls in her slightly weary estuary drawl, before breaking into a laugh. "If you travel at the speed o' light, I s'pose you can expect yer 'at to blow off!" She leans back against the table and folds her arms. "Eh? Anyhow, what're we gonna to do about these turdmunchers? They're just 'opeless, if you ask me. You should be layin' down the law to 'em. Listen, you're no mug. Why do you put up wiv these festerin' idiots? Y'know what? You shouldn't bovver wiv 'em at all. You should say sod 'em and fink about leakin' it. Just go to the TV news guys and tell 'em what's 'appened."

Aysha Malik is an internationally recognised astrophysicist with a PhD in X-ray astronomy and I always treat her advice with the utmost respect and courtesy. "Yeah, yeah, very funny," I snarl. "Shut up, Aysha! You're a totally ignorant blockhead! You know I can't do that."

That may sound rude, but, you see, I don't want to actually *show* her that I respect her, because if I do that, even just once, she'll misinterpret it every time I *dis*respect her and she'll construe it as me being ironic or something. And I don't want her to think that. Wait, yes, no, that's right.

Aysha and I are like two sides of a double-headed coin - very close, but never seeing eye to eye. I suppose you could say we're kind of into each other. But we're too scared to fall too deeply, so we keep each other at a safe distance. I know there's a risk that this may result in one of us pulling away a little and the other pulling away a little bit more until we end up being miles apart and we stop communicating altogether. We're two pieces of a jigsaw puzzle, not necessarily adjacent, in fact not even necessarily belonging to the same puzzle. Anyway, it's worked for us so far. And today we really need to present a united front. Mindful of this, we stroll into the specially-convened crisis meeting in the main focus chamber of the observatory, dissing each other and putting each other down. It's the sixth crisis meeting of the week and hopes of a resolution are almost certain to be dashed before the servbot arrives with the coffee. It's so annoying when that happens. Mind you, the coffee is usually as bad as the smell emanating from the half-open toilet door at the far end of the room.

As we take our seats, a woman with a razor-textured asymmetric bob and a pair of lab-grown purple leather trousers shoots us a look of, well, utter disdain I suppose. Then she resumes her rapid monologue: "On the assumption that we release this information, I need to complete an ETI Disclosure Impact Assessment, so..."

Gene Taylor interrupts her: "Well, that's an assumption you simply shouldn't make!" he says, turning his head to one side so that his colleagues in Scientific Platforms and Communication Strategy can see him rolling his eyes. "You're Head of External Relations. Disclosures are what you do. But right now…" He pauses to fix her with a steely glare. "We're *not* going to release any information!"

Unperturbed, the purple trousers woman reads from her carpalcomm (or CC as most people now refer to them), "Given incontrovertible proof of ETI contact, communication to third parties will be managed by the External Relations Department."

Here we go. I've probably heard enough already. The same old baiting, the same old finger pointing, the same old predictable bla bla bla.

Taylor spreads his palms in a gesture of mock conciliation. "Hey, take it easy there. Do we really need to start quoting chapter and verse? I'm just telling you…"

"And I'm telling *you*," the purple trousers woman interrupts, "we have a protocol document, signed by your superior, applicable to all episodes of this nature. It's official, it's bona fide, and it's the truth." She slaps the table in front of her.

One of Taylor's colleagues passes him a palmpad and he reads from the screen: "Communication to third parties may only be permitted in strict accordance with the security measures specified in the WSC ETI guidelines, section 8, sub-paragraph 14B. Failure to comply with this section shall be punishable by…" The palmpad inexplicably dies. "Anyway, there's not going to be any disclosure," Taylor insists. Forced to think for himself, he resorts to a bit of bluff and bluster. "According to the WSC Space Settlements Act, um, it's a mandatory provision that, er, any disclosure of extraterrestrial communication must be, er, authorised at the highest level and, er, this implements and invokes, you know the thing, whatever." He's apparently trying to cite a higher authority but obviously can't think of anything persuasive or, indeed, genuine. Not off the top of his head anyway.

The purple trousers woman wades in for the kill. "What about the First Protocol itself? The First Protocol stipulates that 'a response to a signal or other evidence of extraterrestrial intelligence may be sent once international consultations have taken place.' So, obviously, we have to go public and organise international consultations. We must seize the day! Carpe diem!"

"There's not going to be any disclosure!"

"There is!"

"No, there isn't!"

The purple trousers woman leans forward and lowers the pitch of her voice to an almost inaudible murmur. "Barba tenus sapientes!" she sneers, stroking an imaginary beard in a gesture of mockery and contempt. So, my guess is, she said something in Latin about beards. Do I sound fed up and bored? Yeah, it's more boring than a thing that's, y'know, uh, nearly as boring as this. Listen, there *aren't* many things as boring as this, so don't have a go at me for not thinking of an actual example.

The bearded Taylor knits his brows in furious embarrassment. "There's not going to be any disclosure!"

"Yes, there is!"

"No, there isn't!"

At this point, I decide I've heard enough. I cough loudly and get to my feet. "Okay, that's it," I say emphatically.

"Yes!" Aysha whispers, far too audibly. "Get in!"

Of course, as soon as I stand up and speak, I'm already regretting it. Sometimes the impatience and frustration just gets the better of me. But we are where we are. I'm on my feet and dozens of pairs of eyes are scrutinising me intently. So what exactly do I say? The best I can come up with is: "Now listen, I'm going to tell you all a story." Really? A story? Is that the *best* I can come up with?

"Really?" says Aysha in an exasperated undertone. "A story? Is that the best you can come up wiv?" Sometimes we're so much on the same wavelength that we could definitely produce polyphonic sound, like, um, two peas in a pod - well, you know, a music studio pod.

I can feel a deep blush creeping up my face like a thermometer on a hot day. "So it was, uh, a manic day at the, um, Scottish patent office," I stammer. "Two men, have both, er, filed applications for the same invention." I tell myself to keep going, because some flickers of relevance will surely, eventually, intuitively occur to me. After all, I'm a smart guy – I've just got to trust in my mental agility and it'll all just fall into place. "They, er, they've both invented the same, uh, windscreen washer system," I continue, praying that a brilliant allegory will simply materialise like one of those old twentieth century photographs in a darkroom tray. "Um, so yeah, these two guys, er, Jamie McSquirter and, um, Rab Nozzle, with these windscreen washer systems - you know, identical in all but name. And, uh, they agree to share credit for the invention, but they just can't agree on a name for it."

"So what happens?" Taylor asks. There's a hint of derision, barely masked. "Is there a point to this?"

"Well, no, nothing happens," I mutter, mainly because I can't think of a witty riposte, "except that the, uh, the examiner can't decide on a name either."

Aysha's head is in her hands. Taylor exchanges looks with the purple trousers woman who parrots his question: "So what happens?"

"Nothing," I say. "Which is a shame because it would have been the best windscreen washer system ever." I look around at the array of sardonic expressions. "Ever!" I repeat for maximum effect.

I reckon everyone is an utter idiot for two minutes every single day of their lives. The secret is to avoid exceeding this limit. I do wish I could heed that adage occasionally. Needless to say, however, I keep talking. Or at least I would do if Aysha doesn't tug my tunic, forcing me to sit back down.

"Shuddup, Neil, for pity's sake," she hisses.

Ignoring her, I stand up again and deliver an impassioned, if massively inarticulate, monologue about the goals and objectives of the RECONNECT project. I appeal to everyone to look beyond the tasks and assignments and protocols and communication strategies that define and confine their sensibilities and I dare everyone to consider the sublime immensity of the universe and the wonderful mysteries it may reveal to us. No wonder Aysha delivers a sharp kick to my ankle.

As I pause for breath, Taylor says, "That's all very well, Neil, but not everyone buys into your grandmother's account of what happened to her."

You can imagine my bewilderment. "So why are you here?" I ask in sheer confusion and disbelief.

"I'm a leading expert in translational informatics in the field of corporate social responsibility," says Taylor, looking slightly aggrieved, "and I build collaborations and provide legislative counsel across all the expert functional divisions. What do you mean, why am I here?"

"So what about, y'know, communicating with extraterrestrials?" My cheeks start to flush again as the exasperation rises. "Y'know? The whole damn point of this whole damn thing?" In the corner of my eye, I notice Aysha pursing her lips and nodding in approval. "What about the damn message we just got from another damn world, millions of light years away from here? How do you legislate for that? Don't you feel a social responsibility to find a way of collaborating with this being from some functional division on the other side of the universe? Hey, whoever this alien guy is, he's asked us a question. The least we can do is have the courtesy to send him a damn reply!"

"Not verified," says Taylor, shaking his head. "We haven't eliminated the possibility of an anomaly in the interpretation of the signal using the Shostak-Hawking Method. It hasn't yet been corroborated empirically by the people at the Michelson Institute." He turns to the purple trousers woman. "And that is precisely why we can't release the data we have!"

At this point, Aysha grabs my sleeve and we leave the room.

"Complete waste o' time!" she says. "You can't reason with these people."

I shrug. "I'll tell you something my grandmother told my dad. I'll have to paraphrase, but it went something like this: the Mortians…" I glance at Aysha. "You know what I'm talking about, right? Mortians?"

Aysha nods.

"Well, the Mortians refer to our planet as the Pale Blue Dot."

"Yeah," says Aysha. "That early astronomer guy, Carl Sagan, used the same description."

It's my turn to nod. "Well, I imagine when you look at Earth from the perspective of outer space, it must make all our earnest politics look pretty damn petty and whiny and inconsequential. You want to grab someone like Taylor by the scruff of the neck and drag him out there into space and say, 'Look, you son of a bitch! Just look!'"

Aysha nods. Tell you what, we're going to be doing some serious formation nodding if this carries on, possibly in time to music, possibly not.

Watery sunshine is half-heartedly threatening to dissolve the lead-grey clouds, while thin wisps of rain scatter in alarm. The trees and shrubbery stir faintly in the strong breeze. You may be wondering how I know this, since the entire facility is located deep below the ground. Well, in the interests of the morale and mental wellbeing of the personnel, live images from CCTV cameras above ground are streamed onto screens embedded along the corridors.

Aysha grabs a couple of flasks of coffee from a passing servbot and we perch on a bench at one of the junctions of the indoor canal system. "We've got to do something about all this," I insist. I've worked myself up into a bit of a frenzy and I want to rant about things for a good while longer. "It's got to stop! Don't you agree? We need to be moving on and we've just got to stop all this infernal delay and procrastination!"

"Hmm, okay," says Aysha. "But let's leave it till tomorrow. Tomorrow mornin', first thing. For now, let's grab somethin' to eat and watch a film."

There is no way she can miss my look of irritated distress.

"I'm so 'ungry I could eat an 'orse. And that puts me in mind of a story. It was a manic day at the Scottish racin' stables…"

"What the hell?"

"Yeah," she continues. "Two men, have both, er, discovered a performance enhancin' diet for race'orses. Their names are Lou Saddle and Jock E. Felloff and they agree to share credit for the new diet. Lou wants it to be called a stable diet, but Jock…"

"What the hell?"

"Yeah, well, I'm jus' tryin' to tell you as gently as I can that *I* am 'ungry and *you* need to work on yer allegories," she says, bitterly. "What was it again? Jamie McSquirter and who?"

"Rab Nozzle."

"Yeah."

The food bar has an extensive selection of salads and we decide to share a carton of jellyfish on a bed of modified eucalyptus leaves. On our way to the 4DX room, we set the ambience parameters for the film. In the circumstances, given a choice between watching the latest Jab Demons action movie or a 4DX remake of Close Encounters of the Third Kind, you'd think we'd go for the Spielberg remake, wouldn't you? You'd be wrong – we choose Jab Demons.

I pay no attention to the film whatsoever. Instead, I think of all the stuff I *should* have said in the meeting. By the time the end credits roll, I put together an absolute killer of a speech, one in which I set out the true priorities for the project in clear, unambiguous terms. I imagine my words liberating everyone in the room from the noose of red-tape that pulls tighter and tighter around their necks and they emerge from their entangled, innovation-strangling mesh of bureaucracy and happily focus their intellectual energy on the bigger issue – configuring the transponder for two-way communication. There's no doubt about it, it would have been the defining moment of my career – uplifting, inspiring, transformative, the last word in motivational speaking. Too bad I've thought about it just over two hours too late.

"What do you suppose happened in the meeting after we left?" I ask Aysha, as we remain seated in the dark.

She casts me a look that says, "Stop fretting. Oh, and stop being such a pain in the butt. And while you're at it, wipe that jellyfish oil off your chin!" When she finally decides to let her vocal chords do the talking, she says, "Okay, let's find out. I've got an audio transcript of the meetin' downloaded on my CC. This app is so cool. See, it translates on the fly! Any language you care to specify. It's uh, configured for French at the minute."

"Why?" I ask.

"I couldn't figure out the configuration thing."

"Well, do you understand French? Can you translate it?"

"I'll try." Aysha listens intently to a female voice, probably belonging to the purple trousers woman.

I interrupt. "Hang on, Aysha. What's that woman's name?"

"Hinton Blewitt," Aysha replies, frowning as she concentrates on the audio recording. "She's the

Head of External Relations. You may not 'ave encountered 'er before now because she's been battlin' long-term depression and consequently 'as 'ad a lot of time off work."

"Hinton Blewett? Isn't that a place somewhere between Bath and Weston-Super-Mare? Why doesn't anyone name their kids Alan or Jane any more?"

Aysha wags a finger at me. "Ssh!" she hisses. "I'm trying to translate this." She pauses the recording and says, "Probleme tres important - it's a very important problem and, uh, wait, did she say 'balayer'? So, uh, I insist on sweeping it under the armpits." Shaking her head, Aysha abandons her doughty attempt at translation and points at my face. "Wipe that jellyfish oil off yer chin!" she says.

THIS WAY UP

If you didn't know her better, you'd think Aysha had a very jaundiced view of humanity. We're sitting with Hinton Blewitt, drinking cocktails in the cornily-named Mars Bar, discussing the benefits of public engagement. It's a subject about as close to my heart as my toenails are. Frankly, if there's one word in the political lexicon guaranteed to make my eyes glaze over, it's public engagement. Okay, that's two words, but you get what I mean. Anyway, I'm letting Aysha do the talking and she's not exactly endearing herself to the Head of External Relations.

"Let's be perfickly honest 'ere," she says, pausing to sip at her Nebula cocktail. "What diff'rence does it make anyway? They'll make an unbeleeevable song 'n' dance about it in the meedja for a couple o' weeks, then everyone'll settle down to normal life, receivin' and dispatchin' drones, watchin' football and talkin' 'bout football on social meedja."

With a quizzical arch of her impeccably manicured left eyebrow, Hinton leans back on her cushioned floaty and speaks slowly in a languid, emotionless monotone, "It's more important than you think. If the expenditure on this project ever becomes public knowledge… well, let's just say we need good publicity and we need positive results to justify our funding requests. Yes, above all, we need to get the public onside." She takes a slow sip from her glass of iced water (she isn't drinking cocktails on account of her medication) and closes her eyes for a few seconds.

"You only need to get the top social meedja gurus onside," argues Aysha. "And you External Relations guys already 'ave 'em in your pockets. As for the general public – it's like 'erdin' sheep. For decades now, the ejoocation system has dumbed 'em down and made 'em feel good wiv meaningless qualifications. Made 'em employable enough to get jobs servicing 3D printbots or dispatchin' drones, but not smart enough to string sentences togevver and fink for 'emselves. See, they don't need to fink for 'emselves cuz the government wants to do all the finking for 'em."

I fink, sorry, I think about voicing my dissent, but then, suddenly, I don't.

Hinton turns to me. "You need to understand," she says, "the energy costs of transmitting a signal with an acceptable signal-to-noise ratio are huge, way beyond what we can meet within our current budget. We have to go cap in hand to the WSC Treasury Department. That's by no means a given. And I'm sure I don't have to remind you, tempus fugit!"

I have to admit, I'm surprised to hear this. It never occurred to me that, in these days of fusion power plants, energy costs might be an obstacle to communication with extraterrestrial intelligence.

We order another round of drinks. It's retro night at the Mars Bar - well, twentieth century night to be precise. The lights are getting dimmer, the music louder and the atmosphere livelier. A servbot is programmed to behave like a twentieth century DJ, complete with a couple of decks, fake vinyl and, yes, a neon bowtie. The bar servbots are clad in dayglo blue and the floor pumps out songs by Procol Harum, Ultravox and Status Quo. Let's face it, it's really naff. I would have preferred to spend the evening keeping the faith, listening to the white label rarities at the Orbit Club in the northern end of the observatory complex, but Aysha and I had to respect Hinton's wishes if we wanted to make her acquaintance.

After a while, Aysha and Hinton disappear to the ladies room, so I join Gene Taylor at the bar. He leans close enough for me to smell the booze on his breath. He's clearly seen too many Lunar Eclipses – the alcoholic kind. "I don't want to aggrovise, eggra…, uh, annoy you," he slurs drunkenly, gesturing with a straw, "but, despite everything you've told us about your grandmother's experiences, we have to bear in mind that the Martians, uh, Mortians may or may not be a benign and benevolent race. Clearly, they have powers beyond our own understanding." Tapping the sleeve of my tunic with his straw, he looks around as if he's about to divulge something confidential. "The thing is, Neil, contact between different races topically, talcum, talcaply, uh, typically works out dysentery, sorry, dastardlously - well that's to say, very badly for the less techno-o-o-logically advanced people." He leans forward too far and slips off his stool. Pretending it's deliberate, he places an arm around my shoulder and continues, "Take the indignious, uh, indigenary, sorry, native tribes of the Caribbean after Columbus landed there.

Now theirs was a very unhappy fate, wasn't it? Wasn't it!"

At this point, out of the corner of my eye, I become aware of a disheveled but beautiful young woman picking herself up off the floor behind us. I've no idea how she got there. She's wearing a bright yellow sweatshirt and black jogging bottoms and her long brown hair spills down over her face from a messy bun.

"Are you okay?" I ask.

Staggering to her feet, she peers at me through her hair and says, "I fell out of a car?" It definitely sounds like a question. "But don't worry, I'm okay." Noticing my perplexed expression, she clarifies, "It was, uh, a parked car. No injuries."

I glance at Taylor, but he's busy performing the hazardous task of getting himself back on his bar stool.

"Have you seen my hat?" the woman asks.

"Um, no, did you have one?" I reply. I suppose it's a bit of a superfluous question - if she's mislaid her hat, she must have had one. The thing is, she's making me feel uncomfortable, not least because she's staring at me, for one moment like a snake ready to strike, and the next moment with an expression that says 'Do I really want to eat that?' A few seconds pass but it feels more like half an hour, so I break the silence and offer to buy her a drink. "I'm Neil, by the way," I tell her.

"Yes, I know," she says in a matter-of-fact tone. "I've been looking for you." These words are accompanied by a thumbs-up and a conspiratorial wink. "And thank you, I'll have, uh, whatever you're drinking. Do you want to share it?"

Taylor decides something weird and flirty is going on, so he leans over to dig his elbow in my ribs, only to lose his balance and fall to the floor. As we pick him up, the woman touches his beard with a couple of exploratory fingers. Now that's rather bizarre, isn't it? I notice a few things about her – she is definitely very attractive, has several coiled pieces of wire in the conch part of her left ear and a small tattoo on the back of her neck which I swear says 'This way up'.

"Did you say you've been looking for me?" I ask.

"Of course!" she says. "For one thing, I was hoping you'd know where my hat is. I hope that answers your question. Verily."

"Verily?" Taylor chortles like a hyena with asthma. Spotting Hinton and Aysha emerging from the ladies room, he slopes away with a rolling gait (also like a hyena) in the opposite direction, slopping his drink all over the floor.

Aysha and Hinton stop and talk to a colleague, leaving me alone for a while with the strange but engaging young woman, but eventually they join us at the bar. I try to introduce the woman, but of course I don't know her name. "So, Aysha, Hinton, this is… uh, I don't, uh… we're just, you know, hanging out." I don't know why I say that.

The woman smiles sweetly. "Oh, great, are we hanging out already?" she says. "Anyway, please excuse me, I need to use the facilities."

"Better warn you," says Aysha. "There's no toilet roll."

The woman smiles. "That's okay, I don't use it." It isn't just *my* jaw that hits the floor like a dead pigeon falling from the top of the Burj Khalifa skyscraper. "Anyway," she continues, "I just want to washen my teeth."

Aysha, Hinton and I look at each other with expressions ranging from puzzlement and amusement to sheer incredulity. Before we have a chance to speak, the woman spins on her heels and calls out to me, "Are you going to get me some flowers?"

None of us can take our eyes off her as she heads off towards the ladies room. Aysha turns to me. "Well, you're a dark 'orse an' no mistake! So, tell us, who's your new girlfriend? And, uh, why is she brushin', oh no, sorry, *washenin'* 'er teeth?"

I roll my eyes in surly disapproval, but I can't help blushing. Feeling slightly unnerved and disoriented, I stare across the room, wondering what the hell has just happened. I've met some eccentric people in my time, but this woman takes the biscuit. At first I thought she must be drunk or mad or both, but, despite the fact that she'd apparently fallen over, her balance appears to be perfectly normal and her blue eyes are clear without any sign of that glazed dead dog expression characteristic of drunks. I have to admit I instantly feel a connection with her. But why? Anyway, snapping out of it, I quiz Hinton on the subject of transmission energy costs. Because, you know, that's what you do in these circumstances.

"So tell me why the energy costs of two-way communication are prohibitive," I say. "Because I don't get it. We're in the 2090s and we've got nuclear fusion. I thought… I mean, it's been touted as the great energy panacea. I thought we'd, y'know, nailed it, energy-wise."

"Well, yes," says Hinton, "obviously fusion has had a totally transformative effect on industrial, commercial and domestic consumption, et cetera, et cetera, but this is a whole new ball game."

Aysha explains, "You see, Neil, in order to deliver sufficient concentrated signal flux, you gotta have incredible amounts of radiated energy. Just loads of it. Otherwise you get too much, y'know, propagation loss."

"Do what now?" I ask, revealing a previously unplumbed level of ignorance.

Aysha frowns. "You do wanna hear the science behind this, don't you?"

"I don't think so," I reply. "I mean I thought I did, but…"

Hinton interrupts. "So, basically, we need to generate protons much more efficiently. And then eventually the price will come down."

"Yeah," says Aysha, "but don' worry – we've got several possible solutions."

"Oh good," I exhale in relief. "That's okay then."

"Hmm, that's it – be positive," says Aysha, nodding sagely and smiling like a doting cobra (I'm sure she's patronising me in a rather insulting way right now). "Always think like a proton! Ha ha!"

"So," says Hinton, "it's now all about applying the principles of Occam's razor."

"Occam's what?" I ask, floundering. "You mean we've got to make staff cuts?"

None of us have noticed the reappearance of the 'This way up' woman, but here she is, grinning broadly, with a mouth full of toothpaste foam. "What do you people use to confine the high temperature plasma?" she asks. Or at least I think that's what she asks – I'm more than a little distracted by the foam dribbling down her chin.

Hinton gives the woman a significant look and discreetly gestures at her own chin. Unable to make herself understood, she gestures again, then just arches her left eyebrow slightly and answers the question. "We use anti-helix stellarators," she says. Pointing to her chin once more, she silently mouths the words "You have something here."

"What? Stellarators?" exclaims 'This way up', spraying toothpaste foam everywhere. "Nah! Try pantyke-accelerated proton beams."

Aysha and Hinton exchange a look of bemused astonishment, like two deer caught in the headlights wondering what the pretty bright circles might mean. Recovering her composure, Hinton narrows her eyes slowly. "Who *are* you?" she asks.

For some reason, 'This way up' pointedly ignores Hinton and turns to me with a big foamy smile. "Aren't you going to ask me how my day was?" she asks.

Aysha's pupils dilate. "Yeah," she says, "aren't you gonna ask 'er, Neil?"

There's no doubt about it, I'm picking up some bad vibes from Aysha. Well, they're just lying on the bar, so I kind of scoop them up, pop them in my mouth and chew them around a bit. Okay. I know. Sorry, but this whole experience is feeling weirder and weirder. Aysha's apparently unhappy or annoyed about something. Is it me? Am I behaving strangely, inappropriately or immorally? Is it my fault the woman with the 'This way up' tattoo keeps saying such odd things and directing her oddness at *me*? Mind you, I'm going to be honest here, despite all the bizarre behavior and eccentricities, I feel inexplicably drawn to her.

"By the way," says Aysha, sourly, "there's no such thing as a pantyke."

I try to communicate with her using just eye contact. "In my mind, I'm thinking you're annoyed about something?" I blink.

She stares and blinks back, "Me? In *my* mind, I'm thinking 'what would I be annoyed about?'"

I shoot a meaningful look that says, well, something generally meaningful, but Aysha looks away. It just doesn't work if you have to direct your meaningful looks around corners - the whole conversation soon becomes incoherent and pointless.

Hinton and 'This way up' are having a good chat about something sciencey that I try to follow for a while, but it's all: "Meh meh meh yada yada yada…" to me. Aysha turns round and we resume our eye contact thing.

"Listen," her brown eyes twinkle, "in my mind I'm thinkin' you can do whatever you like with whoever you like, whenever you like. I don't know who this woman is, but you an' I, we're not a thing, so if you feel attracted to her, just go ahead and do whatever."

At the mercy of some impressive contraction furrows, my eyes can't help revealing my confusion: "Yeh, well, in my mind, I don't know *what* to think. This woman has lit something deep inside me. Well, not exactly lit, more like warmed it up a bit, like a nice bowl of soup. Listen, I *know* you and I are not a thing, but I respect you and we're good friends and I don't want to upset you or anything." Yes, I express all of that, just with the eyes!

Aysha's eyelids start batting furiously, "Well, my mind jus' told your mind I'm okay wiv it. Why *wouldn't* I be okay with it? But if you really respeck me, stop makin' eyes at this crazy woman and pay some attention to me for the first time in yer damn life! Because, well… Really? Do I 'ave to spell it out for you? Are you so insensitive that you can't tell? That's right, in my mind, I have feelings for you!"

"What?" my eyes stare, dumbfounded. "No way! My mind doesn't think you mean it!"

"Oh, but *my* mind doesn't think I *have* to *mean* it!" Aysha's eyes are smiling now. No, actually, they're rolling around laughing like the Martians in the ancient 'Smash' instant potato commercial. It could be a trick of the disco lights, but those may be tears of hilarity streaming down her cheeks. "You just don' understand, do you?" she adds. This time it's not just the eyes - she's using her voice.

"Understand what?" I ask, as confused as a penguin in a tree.

"How nuclear fusion actually works," says Aysha, shaking her head.

Time wears on (I wonder why it doesn't wear out completely). There are several things about the evening that I can attribute to one too many drinks, but, to be fair, I don't need cocktails to not understand nuclear fusion. What I *do* remember is 'This way up' wandering around asking random people if they thought her teeth were sparkly. And I distinctly recall the last thing she said before everything turned to fog: "How long do we have to go out together before I get to see your grandmother?" Yes, that is definitely what she said.

MARY POPPINS

I can sleep blissfully through any kind of alarm tone. But this is not an alarm tone. Nor is it a cockerel. Or birdsong or church bells or rush hour traffic or monks singing vespers or morning exercise music or bacon sizzling in a pan. No, I'm woken by a loud whirring, churning, humming, buzzing sound. What the hell *is* that? And why am I on the sofa? And how did I get home from the Mars Bar last night? I tug a cushion over my head, but I can't shut out that infernal noise.

Then I realise I'm not alone. Why would someone else be in my bachelor pad with me? Perhaps I got a bit drunk last night and Taylor got me home and…

but wait, no, Taylor was certainly more drunk than I was.

Throwing the cushion on the floor, I prop myself up and hear a woman coughing in the kitchen area. A woman? Aysha? When I haul myself to my feet and see that my companion is 'This way up', I kind of do a double take and then a triple take and then I decide I should check if I'm dressed. I'm not. Grabbing the cushion, I shout, "Hello!" That isn't loud enough, on account of the noise of the hand-held electric whisk left to its own devices, whirring and rotating slowly on the worktop. I yell once more at the top of my voice, "Hello?"

'This way up' finally notices me and winks. "Ah, there you are," she says. "Tell me, have we been together long enough for you to buy me some shoes?"

"What?" I ask incredulously. "Why? What's happened? Can you please turn that thing off!"

"I don't know how to," says 'This way up'. "I just thought you might like to buy me a present."

"Why? What's going on? What happened last night?"

"Oh, just a pair of cheap shoes will do," she replies. "Last night? We were at the bar, remember?"

I walk over awkwardly, covering myself up as best I can, and switch off the whisk. "Yes, but that's about all I *do* remember."

"Well, we left the bar and then we went to the next level."

I look at her in horror. My mind is like a lorry on black ice, slewing from side to side, oversteering more and more each time until eventually it jackknifes and overturns. "We did?" I exclaim. "I mean did we…? You know. Well, how can I put this? I mean did our, uh, relationship get, y'know, serious? What do you mean by the next level?"

"We're on level two, right?"

The penny drops and I breathe a small sigh of relief. My pad is on the second floor of the observatory complex. "So, we didn't, uh, you know, get intimate or anything?"

"No, no, I don't have the disposition for it," says 'This way up' breezily, walking over to the kettle and cramming two slices of bread in it. "But don't worry – I'm in this for real! You did say relationship, right?"

Obviously, I need to back pedal a little. "Relationship? Yeah, no, I don't… I, uh, you know, I don't think we need to do any labelling yet, do we? Or at all." Okay, at this point, I really don't know what else to say, so I shake my head and make my way to the bedroom to get dressed.

Sitting on the edge of the bed, I flick my CC, scroll to the entry for Aysha and speak into it slowly and hesitatingly, "Hey, how ya doin'? You okay? Um, I don't know what happened last night. I guess I got wasted, cuz, y'know, it's all a bit of a blank. Uh, catch up with you later maybe?" Straight away, I get a 'busy' auto-response – Aysha's configured her CC to bounce messages from me. She's never done that before. I feel a pang of something.

For the very first time, I feel like I've developed an emotional affinity with Aysha. I'd just laugh at the idea if it weren't for the fact that something inside me is hurting. So, is it possible that establishing a connection with 'This way up' may actually be a kind of displacement thing? Could it be that this encounter has activated the AI and ACC subregions of my brain and made me aware that I have feelings for Aysha? No, that doesn't make sense. Perhaps I'm just feeling unaccountably vulnerable and my mind's playing tricks on me. Hmm, I really need to put some trousers on.

Suitably attired, I walk urgently into the kitchen area where 'This way up' is cracking eggs into the toaster.

"When we left the bar last night, was Aysha with us?" I ask. "What exactly happened? Wait, what on earth are you doing with those eggs?"

"No, she left early. Said she had an upset stomach." Pursing her lips, she drops her voice to a repentant murmur. "It's possible… that is, it's quite likely that it may have been me that upset her stomach." As I look at her quizzically and basically just sort of grunt, she goes on, "Well, I told her I didn't think she was fat." I gape at her while she continues: "Hmm? It's true, I *don't* think she's fat. Tell me, why would a stomach get upset about that? Anyway, then I told her you and I had a lot to talk about and she should make herself scarce if she didn't want to play raspberry."

"You did what? Play what?"

"A raspberry. You know – be with two people who would rather be alone."

Changing the subject is the only recourse available to me right now. "Why have you put bread in the kettle and what *are* you doing with those eggs?"

"Oh sorry, are they fertilised?"

"What? Er, no, of course not."

"Well, then, what's the problem? I don't understand. What have unfertilised eggs done to earn dignity? I'm just trying to make you some breakfast. Tell you what, you're going to have to teach me how to use these tools."

"Tools?" I ask, as I absent-mindedly put the kettle under the tap, forgetting that it's stuffed full of bread. "Wait, seriously, what's going on? First of all… uh, yeah, first of all, what's your name?"

"Mary Poppins." Her expression is as impassive as the Sphinx delivering one of its riddles.

"Mary Poppins," I echo lamely. "Right, okay." That's it. I've had enough for the moment and head off to the bedroom once more. After leaving another message for Aysha and immediately receiving another automatic bounce-back, I throw myself onto the bed and do something I'm not used to doing too often – I do some thinking!

What if I'm right and I've developed a thing for Aysha? Could it be it's something that's been slowly building for months, maybe even years, and my conscious mind has just refused to acknowledge it? And it's kind of found a displaced outlet now in the shape of 'This way up', sorry, er, Mary Poppins? I've heard of this before - people displacing their feelings. But usually it's a defensive mechanism whereby someone might, for example, redirect anger from one target to another to avoid consequences - if you're angry with your boss, you may get the sack, so you take it out on someone or something else.

Perhaps *denying* feelings towards Aysha is a defensive mechanism I've developed over time, subconsciously protecting myself from the risk of rejection. Here's another scenario: perhaps it's a slightly different kind of displacement thing, like when you can't have champagne you tell yourself you like prosecco just as much. Anyway, as my ears are suddenly besieged by a noise akin to a pneumatic drill, I think I should be more concerned about what the hell is happening with my kitchen appliances.

I dive out of the bedroom. Thrashing away on the worktop, the food processor is attempting to chop up a can of tuna, still in the can. Mary is studying the fire extinguisher. I notice she's pulled the pin. Suddenly, before I can say a word, she squeezes the trigger and sprays chemical mist randomly in all directions around the room before shrieking in panic and tossing the canister towards me. It crashes onto the kitchen table, launching milk and eggs and orange juice into the air. Much of it spatters all over my trousers and socks. Mary tries to mop up the mess with one of my tunics that was lying folded on a chair, while I rush over to the worktop to switch off the food processor.

When some sort of order is restored, I prop myself against the table and Mary drops into a kitchen chair facing me. Giving myself plenty of time to calm down and consider what I should say, I clear my throat, fix her with a droll expression and tell her, "Please don't tell me that anything can happen if you let it. And please don't tell me that you never explain anything."

Mary bites her bottom lip and shrinks a little in her chair. "I'm not really Mary Poppins," she says.

BLOOD MOON RISING

It may or may not be a coincidence, but tonight sees the final part of the lunar tetrad of 2090-2091 - four successive total lunar eclipses, spaced at six full moons apart. The first Blood Moon eclipse in the series occurred on the night of March 15th 2090. The second one took place on September 8th 2090 and the third one was March 5th 2091. The fourth and final eclipse of the tetrad falls tonight. In the past, people have spoken of a lunar tetrad as representing a fulfilment of biblical prophecy. According to the Book of Joel: 'The sun will be turned to darkness and the moon to blood before the coming of the great and awesome day of Jehovah.' Some still believe that these signs presage climactic events.

I'm not sure if I'm filled with a sense of fear and foreboding or if I expect 'This way up' or 'Mary' (or whatever her name is) to make some kind of earth-shattering declaration, but I hope she can at least divulge her real name and explain a few little things, like why she's wrecked my kettle by boiling it with nothing inside except slices of bread.

"So," she says, studying the tropical fish in my aquarium with absorbed fascination, "you must be wondering who I really am. And why I'm here and what exactly is going on."

"Yep, you could say that."

"You'll have to brace yourself then," she warns, "because I'm going to jump off the deep end without a paddle and I'm not going to save it for a rainy day." All at once a cloud of doubt pirouettes across her face like dry ice on a stage. "Well, I don't know. Maybe it's not the right time. Maybe you're not ready to hear what I have to say. Not just yet."

"Seriously, I'm ready."

Chewing her lip, she looks at me as if she's peering into the depths of my soul and finding nothing but a couple of goldfish. I hope that's not the case. I like to think of my soul as a vast and awesome ocean and deep in the depths of it there's a cave labeled

'Do Not Enter.' Maybe there are no great mysteries hidden behind the entrance to this cave – maybe it's just a kind of underwater laundry and utility room – but there *could* be something lurking in there, you never know. Also, stop tapping the glass!

Anyway, perhaps there's something I can say to encourage or prompt her? Right on cue, I can't think of anything. And I don't know why it comes to my notice at this particular moment, but, hey, it does - not only does this woman talk and act like she's completely deranged, but there's no CC on her wrist. "I knew there was something strange about you," I blurt out. "You're not wearing your CC!"

For a second or two, she seems put out by this. "I'd have worn my CC if I'd wanted to," she asserts, rather defensively. There's something in her demeanour that suggests she doesn't even know what I'm talking about. But surely – no one is ever separated from their carpalcomm, right?

"Don't worry," I tell her, "I'm sure there must be a good reason. I mean, yeah, there must be a reason?"

Our eyes lock. With a barely perceptible shake of the head, she replies cagily, "Is it bad not having a CC?"

"Do you know what I'm talking about? I mean do you even know what a carpalcomm *is*?"

"Yeah, of course, verily."

"Use it in a sentence then."

"It could be that I just can't afford one," she suggests, tilting her head and ignoring my challenge. "Maybe I just don't come from that sort of privileged background. Not everyone has a credit rating, you know."

"Yeah, *I* don't come from a privileged background either, but come on, even really poor people know what a carpalcomm is. In the highly unlikely event that they may not have one, they sure as hell know what it is!"

"Well, if you think that's strange, I don't know, maybe it is. But it's nothing compared to what I'm about to tell you. You'd better sit down. But first, give me those trousers. I'll clean them up for you."

"Promise you won't put them in the food processor or the fish tank," I joke, trying to lighten the mood a little.

There's a knock at the door. Aysha's muffled voice calls out, "Neil! Neil, are you there? Just thought I'd drop by. We've got a conference wiv Taylor and the finance people in twenny minutes. You ready? We can go togevver."

"Just a minute. I'll put some trousers on."

With immaculate timing, 'Mary Poppins' picks that moment to call out, "Hello Aysha!"

Well, that's Sod's Law, I suppose. Obviously, the universe doesn't actually conspire against you. But the way I see it, it doesn't go out of its way to line up the fish when you cast your line either. The silence on the other side of the door is deafening, like standing in a dark forest right after a heavy snowstorm.

"Aysha?" I call, more in horrified regret than in any expectation that she'll answer, or, indeed, still be there. But maybe I'm overthinking this. Aysha's smart – she'll understand what's going on. "Aysha! It's not what it looks like, er, sounds like!"

"Meh, meh, meh," says 'Mary Poppins', studying my face. "Meh, meh, meh, blah, blah." Well, of course she doesn't say that at all. But she may as well have done, for all the notice I take. What she *actually* says is the most staggering, astounding and sensational thing anyone has ever said to me in my entire life. It's a pity I miss it.

But it's difficult to focus on *anything* when you're beset by feelings of loss, horror, failure, guilt, shame, anger, depression, low self-esteem and helplessness. "Sorry, what did you say?" I ask her.

I'm at least *half*-listening when she curtsies elaborately and repeats her apocalyptic message: "I said I'm from Smolin9, the planet formerly known as Morys Minor. My name is yukawa3 and I know your grandmother. I need your help to fulfil my mission."

I've lost count how many times my brain has gone numb this morning. Now it's spinning like a fruit machine and turning up a row of bananas. "Did you just curtsy?" I ask. Well, I know, but, come on, what would *you* have said?

Ignoring my question, 'This way up', sorry, 'Mary Poppins', sorry, yukawa3 frowns and squints at me uneasily. "Did you hear what I said? I'm yukawa3."

"No you're not."

"Sir, do you question an intergalactic emperor?" Yukawa3 put her (his?) hands on his (her?) hips in a gesture of reproach.

"But you're *not* an intergalactic emperor," I point out. "You're just not, *are* you? I mean even if you are who you say you are, you're not an intergalactic emperor." When you're unexpectedly confronted with the most incredible circumstance you've ever encountered, it can be difficult to adjust properly. We all have our own mechanisms for doing this. As for me, I adjust by putting my trousers back on, orange juice splashes and all. "Okay, so… So, first of all, if you're yukawa3, what should I call you?"

Yukawa3's blue eyes blink in genuine surprise. "How about yukawa3?"

"Right," I say, pausing to give myself as much time as possible to get my head around the situation. Unfortunately, there simply isn't enough time in the history of my bit of the universe. "Please, I don't understand what's going on. Something seriously weird is happening and I think I… I don't know what to say. I don't know what to think. How am I supposed to make sense of all this?"

"It's simple," yukawa3 assures me. "You've just got to listen to me."

"I suppose there isn't an alternative way?"

By no stretch of the imagination is yukawa3's introductory spiel a comprehensible and coherent one, but he (she) weaves so much detail into it that my scepticism fades like a cheap pair of jeans. He (she) becomes more and more agitated and excited as he (she) develops his (her) story and concludes with the suggestion that we throw the mother of all parties and invite everyone on the planet.

"No," I tell him.

His (her) face drops like a hiker falling over a cliff. "You don't think we should have a party celebrating my return to the planet?"

"No."

"So no one will make balloon dogs?"

Wow. That's uncanny. "Okay," I relent, without making any allusions to the pink balloon dog of my childhood. "We'll have a party, but it's going to be just you and me. No one else is to find out about this. No one! Understood?"

Disappointment etched across his (her?) features, yukawa3 pouts, crosses her (his?) arms and says, "I don't understand. You've been trying to get hold of me, haven't you?"

"Well, yes," I concede. "And we got the message about your hat. That's not the point. You don't know us well enough. You don't know how people will react to the news of your visit. You have to take into account the danger of promulgating fear among the people on this planet. Once you set certain forces alight, you sometimes have very little control over where they lead. In fact, while we're on the subject, tell me something - how much research did you do before you came here?" I'm starting to see certain things in a different light now – the kitchen appliances, the toilet paper, the tooth-brushing, the absence of a CC, the whole litany of bizarre behaviour.

"I did *plenty* of research," says yukawa3 indignantly. "Plenty. Why do you ask?"

I start listing all her glaring gaffes and faux pas with, I confess, a little too much relish in my voice (by the way, I'm going to stick to calling him her, if you see what I mean).

"Bread in the kettle?" says yukawa3 with a blustering, defensive note in her voice. "What? Seriously? Like nobody's ever made *that* mistake?"

"You say you know who I am. And you say you were trying to use a kind of 'honey trap' to grab my attention?"

Yukawa3 nods. "Well, I didn't want to come back as a penguin again," she says, in reference to a previous ill-fated sojourn on Earth. "Too many traumatic experiences. So yes, a honey trap, and, be fair, it worked really well, didn't it? So my research couldn't have been that bad. Should I cut your toenails now?"

"What?"

Seizing my foot, she starts poking clumsily at my toes with some nail clippers. "It's part of the implementation script. Third stage."

Eventually, I recover my foot, er, both feet, and salvage my dignity. Okay, I know. Creepy? No! Hey, they *needed* trimming. Anyway, right now I need to clarify a whole raft of questions that spring into my mind. "When I first saw you, you were picking yourself up off the floor in the bar. What was that about? What was going on?"

"Uh, I was trying to run up to you with slow motion hair."

I must admit I laugh like a hyena in a drain.

"Well," says yukawa3, "What about *your* pathetic attempts to make contact with *me*? Seriously. What was your strategy? Tape a flyer to a lamppost with a picture of a penguin? Missing – extraterrestrial penguin?" She counters my laughter with a series of exaggerated snorts.

We exchange looks of mutual discombobulation. I point out that the entire CONNECT facility has been dedicated to the search for signals from Smolin9 and other intelligent civilisations.

"Well, you still haven't replied to my text message," she complains.

I can't bring myself to attempt an explanation for our failure to transmit a reply. "We need to give you a proper, uh, earthling name," I declare. "I'm going to call you Catfish."

"Okay. Is that a normal, acceptable earthling female name?"

"Oh yes," I lie. It's actually, of course, a colloquial term for someone who adopts a false identity, especially on Facescreen or other social media, in pursuit of deceptive online romances. It seems appropriate somehow. Now what about a surname? I cast a quick glance around the room and notice my stained clothing. "Uh, tunic. We'll call you Catfish Tunic."

"Okay, I'm Catfish Tunic," says Catfish, offering her hand. "Pleased to meet you. But no party?"

"No party," I confirm. "Oh, actually, now I think about it, there *is* a party tonight to celebrate the blood moon. You can come to that. But it's absolutely imperative you don't tell anyone else who you really are. Not just yet. Got it?"

"Yes, I got it. What sort of party? Is it one of your earthling gatherings where people meet up to see if they can go through several hours without making conversation - playing loud music, cavorting around, getting drunk and laughing all the time about nothing at all? And they video themselves throughout the process to prove their success. Is it one of those? Will I enjoy it?"

"Not with that attitude you won't!" I tell her. But I admit the thought occurs to me that Catfish may have done a little more research than I've given her credit for. "I can't make any promises," I tell her. "It's being organised by Hinton's sister, Disney. I'm in charge of the music, so the playlist is going to be just epic!"

Disney is a biochemist and a clinical investigator in charge of drug trials in the pharmaceutical industry. In her private life, she describes herself as a 'creative visionary'.

Catfish's face lights up a little and then clouds over. "It's not a formal thing is it? There won't be tuxedos, will there? They remind me of penguins."

"Don't worry, it's fancy dress. Very informal."

"Good. So there'll be balloon dogs?" she asks in a distracted sort of way, apparently captivated by the elegant beauty of my tropical fish. "By the way, I'm really hungry."

"I've got to go to a conference. I'll fix some food when I get back. Stay here and don't touch anything. Yeah, please, please don't touch *any* of these electrical appliances!" I get as far as the door, hesitate for a moment and turn round to see Catfish has plunged her head in the fish tank. Okay, maybe this is perfectly regular behaviour on other planets. I guess things are going to be different around here for a while. I shrug my shoulders and make my way to the conference room.

APORIA

I'm late for the conference with the finance department, but I still stop outside the Aporia Conference Room, as I always do, to gaze at the engraved plaque on the wall outside. It depicts a woman with a spear next to a sleeping dragon. Interesting story. In the 2060s, a team of archeologists investigating an ancient burial site on the upper reaches of the River Parrett found several graves containing the bodies of young women alongside weapons such as bows and arrows, quivers and spears. The discovery gave rise to legends of a mythical race of women warriors, the Parretts, who spent their time gathering seeds, fishing, hunting and fighting rival tribes. They used canoes to travel up and down the river. The best known of these legends is undoubtedly the legend of Aporia.

Aporia was the seventh daughter of a seventh daughter. She never went out fishing with her sisters. She rowed around in her own canoe making up wild stories about sea monsters. One day, a real fire-breathing sea dragon emerged from the waves and threatened to set fire to one of the canoes. Legend has it that the dragon couldn't decide which canoe to set ablaze and instructed Aporia to choose. Unable to make up her mind, Aporia hesitated and hesitated until the dragon got bored and fell asleep and they all escaped. To this day, the word aporia is used to refer to a person who hesitates in the face of the enemy. There is a West Country proverb - 'better to be an aporia for a few minutes than dead for the rest of your life'.

The lintel over the door bears an inscription '*dubito, ergo cogito, ergo sum*' (meaning 'I doubt, therefore I think, therefore I am').

I take a seat towards the back and scan the room for a glimpse of Aysha's mane of long brunette hair. I doubt if she's here, therefore I think she's upset, therefore I am too. Surreptitiously, I whisper a quick message into my CC: "Aysha? It's me. Uh, Neil. I'm at the conference. Where are you?" Another automatic bounce-back.

Gene Taylor's closely cropped head is lightly beaded with sweat as he delivers an apparently uncomfortable speech about the need to codify a deal that will ensure the future financial viability of the RECONNECT project. I'm too busy surreptitiously checking my CC for messages from Aysha to follow all the finer points of his argument, but I assume they're as uncompelling as usual. I don't know if Taylor will clinch a deal here today or not. And frankly I don't care. I can't help it – I've allowed my spirits to sink into bottomless indifference. Later in the bar, Taylor will talk, as he always does, about surviving a knife-edge, cliff-hanging drama consisting of threats and counter-threats, concessions offered and refused, promises made and broken. But the truth is, this monthly farce is nothing but institutional uselessness, a choreographed charade in which the final outcome has already been agreed in smoke-filled rooms days before. It's a pantomime in which the characters slapstick their failure to reach mutual agreement before dramatically turning everything on its head and finishing with a big song and dance number about nothing in particular. Clearly, I've attended too many of these finance conferences and I've become jaundiced.

Time goes by like treacle flowing uphill. Just as my mind starts drifting to thoughts of tonight's music, I get a message on my CC. It's Aysha! Translating voice to text, I study the words carefully: "Sorry, couldn't make the conference. Something cropped up. Hope you found some trousers. See you tonight at the Blood Moon Party?" Several nuanced interpretations later, I conclude that everything's okay and there won't be any awkwardness tonight. Well, at least she's talking to me anyway.

If you're wondering why finance appears to play such an important role in all our activities on the project, here's an enlightening fact about RECONNECT - it comes under the auspices of the Enterprise and Industry Directorate of the WSC, suggesting, you have to agree, that there's a hell of a lot of focus on the potential economic benefits of contact with extraterrestrial life. Far too much focus, you might think. I know I do. Ever since my grandmother's story broke in the late 80s and was given credence by the mainstream media making the connection with the extraordinary appearance of the Voyager probe on the White House lawn earlier in the century, a lot of the forward-thinking players in the powerful tech megacorporations have been simply dying to get their hands on technology such as microwockys, biomimetic mutators, superluminal communication and wormhole travel. They don't give a damn about any wider agenda. It's all about money.

I can't help feeling that if I were to stand up and announce that there's an extraterrestrial visitor pretty much wrecking my apartment right above their heads, they'd just shrug and carry on talking about impact investment and bottom-up budgeting.

My mind's been wandering so much, I nearly miss my cue – we've arrived at the part of the meeting where I'm scheduled to make my contribution. I rise to my feet to deliver my pitch about revisions of the strategic plan. Determined to be on message, quick on my feet, charismatic and genial, I make a great start by dropping my palmpad. Before I have any chance to rescue it, it hops and skitters across the floor and eventually vanishes through a gap next to the skirting board, while I just look on in horror. You know what? I think I've had enough today. Actually, yes, I think I'm officially going to cross over to the dark side – I feel like I could draw a lot of freedom and power from the dark emotions I feel right now.

So here's the thing - I've got to make a persuasive pitch for increased funding off the top of my head without the elaborately constructed presentation that's just disappeared under the floorboards. Terrific. It was challenging enough before this happened. Obviously, yes, I know - it's all completely ridiculous and irrelevant now yukawa3 has turned up. Nevertheless, I'm here in my role as head of a commission to secure money for the development of transponder modifications and associated transmission techniques. Public interest in the project has been waning, but I'm under strict instructions not to divulge any information relating to yukawa3's message. Once again I say it – terrific!

After outlining the costs involved in transmitting a signal and after refreshing everyone's memory about my grandmother's experiences and the Voyager White House incident, I'm really scraping the barrel. I need to beef it up with something more emotive and visionary.

"As you all know, this project has always been my dream," I declare. "I've dedicated my life to making contact with extraterrestrial life. I won't give up on this dream and I'll work day and night to make it come true."

Some chinless wag in the section occupied by the Treasury wizards calls out, "Well, you'll *need* to work nights if you're gonna be dreaming!"

Ignoring him, I really start to get my oratory thing going: "Here on the RECONNECT project, we intend to venture forth with an open mind and an open heart in the quest for knowledge about extraterrestrial life so that we may inspire and guide future generations. I personally have a passion for discovery and I intend to push the envelope and guide the world towards the beckoning frontier of intergalactic space. I aspire to make the world a *bigger* place – a world comprising not just this one small planet but entire galaxies. And I will persevere until people respond to my dream on a truly emotional level; until it dazzles and dumbfounds them and tears them apart and they shout and cry out with rapture and torment…"

The chinless heckler in the Treasury section interrupts me. "Keep that up and you won't have to persevere much longer," he says. "You're tormenting me already!"

Uh oh. My hackles are rising quickly and my mind's running wild. "Well, you can mock all you like, but what if I was to tell you that something astonishing has already actually happened?" I begin, nodding defiantly. Then I notice my wrist is flashing. Taylor's voice issues from it in a feverish whisper, "Don't! Just don't!" Glancing over at him, I notice he's looking very agitated, his face contorted over his CC. I continue, slightly more tentatively, "What if I were to tell you there's been a development?"

"No!" rasps Taylor into his CC in such a loud, hoarse whisper that heads start turning towards him. "If you don't shut up right now, I'm going to come straight over and knock some sense into you!" Feeling the pressure of dozens of pairs of eyes on him, he looks up sheepishly and mumbles, "Sorry, er, yeah, it's my wife. Always wanting another pair of shoes!" He probably should have left it there, but Taylor, aware that no one seems to be too impressed with his attitude towards his wife, is clearly unaware of the first law of holes - when you're in one, stop digging. "I'm only kidding, baby, honey," he tells me, purring into his CC. "Of course you can have the shoes. Anyway, gotta go. I'm in a meeting." Unfortunately for him, several people have noticed by now that his voice is coming from two places at once – his mouth and my CC.

Actually, this is one of the few times I want Taylor to keep talking. No, not because I like hearing him call me 'baby' and 'honey', but because I would really like to avoid continuing with my presentation. Anyway, mercifully, that's exactly what Taylor does – talk, talk, talk. More droning and wittering about intraday momentum patterns and smart beta strategies.

Still, it gives me an opportunity to reflect. So that's what I do. I reflect on my friendship with Aysha. And I reflect on the staggering fact that yukawa3 is here on this planet, in this building, actually in my apartment waiting for me. And I reflect on our civilisation's deep ambivalence towards contact with extraterrestrial life.

Back in the second half of the last century, governments used to spoon-feed gullible ufologists a regular diet of lies and half-truths - Roswell, Area 51, flashing lights, flying hub caps, 'evidence' of alien abductions, etc, etc - knowing their fertile imaginations would happily divert attention away from military top-secret technology. Test pilots flying experimental silent helicopters, for example, later openly admitted attaching flashing lights to their craft to fool civilians. The resulting conspiracy-theory smoke and mirrors served to obscure genuine incidents like the Apollo 10 astronauts hearing "space music" while they were orbiting the moon in May 1969. Consequently, here we are, over a hundred years further on and we still don't know how to release information about extraterrestrial life into mainstream consciousness. And we're not even sure if we should.

The door opens and Catfish stands there, holding an egg between thumb and forefinger.

"Excuse me," says the chinless guy. "Who are you? What are you doing here?"

Ignoring him, Catfish waves at me. "Neil! I've been looking everywhere for you! Listen, I've worked out how to cook these things. Only, it was starting to get cold so I thought I'd better bring it over to you."

The chinless guy regards both of us with thinly disguised hostility. "This conference is limited to personnel who have level four security clearance. Kindly identify yourself!"

"I'm Catfish Tunic," says Catfish with a smile that's hard to define. "I hope that answers your question."

Okay, now I'm beginning to regret coming up with that name. It doesn't sound too authentic right now.

"Do you even work here?" asks the chinless guy.

"Uh, no," replies Catfish carelessly. "I'd consider it, but, honestly, the salary sucks. I just share an apartment with Neil."

Completely nonplussed, Taylor pitches in: "I don't know what's going on here. But let's be clear about one thing. The observatory accommodation is only available to employees of the facility and financiers on secondment from the WSC Treasury Department."

As impassive as you like, Catfish says, "Okay, well, in that case I guess I can start today."

"Don't be ridiculous," says the chinless guy, "You need to have qualifications from the Chartered Institute!"

"This world is so unfair!" Catfish complains, "The unqualified are constantly being discriminated against."

The chinless guy takes it on himself to eject her from the room. He marches across and seizes her arm.

Catfish remains as impassive as Rodin's Thinker contemplating the ironing. "Wait," she says, "I *am* actually very well qualified. I ran the equity derivatives division at Douche Bank."

"You mean Deutsche Bank?" asks the chinless guy, hesitating for a moment.

"Yeah, er, that's the one. I made an absolute mint for them."

"So why did you leave? Did you get fired?"

"Of course not."

"So why did you leave?"

Catfish looks perplexed, so I do my best to salvage her story: "Well, er, the mint she made got sucked into a Ponzi scheme and her bonuses got sucked into a vortex of, uh, disappearing money. And she decided to join a rock band instead."

"What? A rock band?"

"It was a cry for help," says Catfish. Clearly, we're both struggling to maintain any semblance of plausibility by now.

"So what did you do?" asks the chinless guy, slightly mesmerised despite himself.

"I tried actually crying for help," she replies, making sad eyes at him.

Snapping himself together like someone coming out of a trance, the chinless guy pushes her towards the door. "That's enough!" he snaps, "Out! You're just talking crap! You've no right to be here! Shove off!"

I hurry over towards them and he glares at me before releasing Catfish from his grasp. "Hey, there's no need to act like a jerk," I tell him. "Leave her alone! Come on, Cat, let's get out of here."

He launches a bit of a sweary tirade at me. I don't often lose my cool, but it's kind of been one of those days. I turn around and snarl, "Bit of a personal question, but did your chin get sick of being so close to all the crap you talk and just disappear?"

What really impresses me is the restraint being shown by Catfish during this altercation. Then I notice – perched precariously on the ginger fringe covering the chinless guy's forehead is a small coronet of broken eggshell. The yolk dribbles slowly onto his eyebrows and down his nose.

Oh well, so much for my breakfast.

BITTER FRUIT

"I told you to stay put," I remind Catfish as we traverse the corridors on our way back to my pad. "You do realise that didn't exactly go very well?"

"Could have been worse," she says. "No one got phasered."

"Phasered?"

"Yeh, that guy was starting to annoy me. I've got a proton phaser in my bag, disguised as a hairbrush."

"Wait a minute", I object. "You people can disguise yourselves as other beings and you've mastered wormhole travel, but your weapon of choice is a hairbrush?"

Obviously I'm being tongue-in-cheek, but for a moment Catfish looks offended. "Well," she says, "These weapons may be a little dated now, but they still, you know, terminate people. I've never heard anyone who's been terminated complaining."

"Okay, listen," I blow out a breath. "We need to establish a few ground rules. A *lot* of ground rules. I'm going to have to tutor you. God knows, it's going to be really challenging trying to pass you off as one of us. It's going to be like mixing oil and water."

Catfish interrupts. "Yes, I'm trying to learn already. Some of your language structures confuse me. Oil and water. Is that a mixed metaphor?"

"What? No, a mixed metaphor is a combination of metaphors that don't work well together."

"So, oil and water work well together?"

"No, no, oil and water are immiscible. They can't be blended."

"Right," says Catfish, nodding in doubtful comprehension. "They don't work well together."

"No."

"Like a mixed metaphor?"

"Yes. No!" I sigh in exasperation. "Anyway, it wasn't a metaphor – it was a simile! Look, all I'm trying to say is you've got to keep a very low profile until such time as you learn how to behave. And I'd appreciate it if we could, you know, set the bar a little higher than no one got phasered!"

"Okay, well then no one got smited."

"Smited?"

"Verily. I could have smited him."

"Will you please quit it with all the phasering and smiting! No one uses that word anyway. And I don't think it's 'smited' - it's 'smote'!"

"Smote?"

"The past tense is smote. Stop! I can't believe this conversation."

We both gather our thoughts for a moment. The corridor screens reveal a succession of images from the gardens above ground. The ambience is enhanced by the sound of water spouting from a statue of a serpent-like dragon. It cascades dramatically into the ornamental lake. I imagine riding a dragon on the raging sea. I don't know why. Maybe it's… no, I simply don't know why.

The lake languishes in neglect in the overgrown gardens. Beyond it is a statue of Nicnevin standing in splendid isolation in the middle of an orchard of small, disfigured trees shedding blushing red, heart-shaped apples. According to West Midlands folklore, Nicnevin, the Queen of the Fairies, discovered a crown made of gossamer on a hillside. The story was immortalised in a song written by Robert E. Kahn:

The Queen of the Fairies sang so sweet
As she danced on the haunted hill:
'Behold the crown lying at my feet,
In this winter morning's chill.'

I can't remember the rest of it. Anyway, the crown was snatched from her by Hecate, the goddess of witches, who aspired to be the Queen of the Fairies herself and was jealous of Nicnevin. The tears rolled down Nicnevin's cheeks, dropped to the earth and turned into heart-shaped apples. This rare fruit still grows wild in places like Warwickshire and the Brendon Hills in Somerset. It tastes very bitter and some locals refuse to eat it, insisting that the juice from the apples actually consists of Nicnevin's tears. Most locals, however, are less circumspect and will gladly sell you a basket of bitter-tasting apples at roadside stands and farmers' markets. Just thought I'd warn you.

I researched this story a little while back and discovered that Nicnevin is a name of Gaelic origin, so I don't know what happened there – I guess she must have been on holiday in Hinckley at the time.

Back in my apartment, we sit down, drink coffee and stare at each other as if we're using telepathy, but, quite frankly, if Catfish is using telepathy, her thoughts are really dull and unimpressive and, I would have to say, a pretty poor advert for extraterrestrial civilisation.

She breaks the silence. "Well, I'd better tell you about my mission," she says, biting her bottom lip.

"Yeah," I agree. "You better had. I'm dying to know what you're here for. Are you studying us again like smolin9 did? And reporting back to the mothership, er, mother planet, whatever? Are you all thinking of coming over and colonising Earth? Something like that?"

"No, of course not," she says, "We don't have imperial ambitions. This is not about intergalactic hegemony. We're not like that."

"You've got a phaser thing," I point out.

"Yes, but that's not what we're about. We'll only phaser and smite people if they offer resistance. No, no, sorry, that came out wrong. It was a joke. Ha ha ha ha ha. A joke. Let's break eggs together in honour of peace."

"Okay, go ahead, tell me your mission. It's not really about the hat, is it?" Between you and me, there may be a hint of an eye-roll.

"No," she says without hesitation. And then she hesitates. And bites her bottom lip again. "Well, not entirely. I *would* quite like it back if you can get it for me."

Knowing full well the sou'wester is securely ensconced in the Smithsonian Museum of American History, I slowly shake my head and carefully break the bad news.

"It's a very important hat," says Catfish, looking more than a little vexed. "It has symbolic value. It represents the spirit of mutual respect and dialogue and creative hat-sharing between diverse planetary civilisations. It's…"

"It's only a hat! I can get you another one."

"Only a hat? You just said yourself – your people have put it in the Smithsonian Museum of American History. So I'm assuming that hats are as important in your culture as they are in ours. Hats represent authority and power and, because they cover the head, they epitomise thought, wisdom and knowledge." Catfish seems to be unusually lucid, probably because she's reciting something she's memorised. "Hats can represent ideologies and give you an intuitive sense of what a person is all about. Exchanging and sharing hats is a mark of homage, a way of paying respects to fellow beings. I think we both know the significance of that hat."

"Okay, so maybe it's significant and symbolic and it represents stuff and all the rest of it... but, wait, come on, have you seriously just come back here to fetch your hat?"

Catfish purses her lips and scratches her head. "Er, no," she says. "Well, not officially anyway." Realisation dawns on her. "Sooooo, you can't get the hat? Oh my god. Oh my god." As she takes her hand from her head, a clump of brown hair comes away with it.

Staring at the severed hair, I ask, "What's going on?"

"Nothing," she responds. "What? Has *your* hair never fallen out? Stop staring!" Suddenly, she flicks her wrist and the hair scatters across the room. "Ugh, lice! Can't stand lice! Ugh!"

"Lice? What do you mean? You haven't got lice. What's happened to your hair?" I really feel quite concerned about her. "Is that why you need your hat?"

"Okay, between you and me, maybe these biomimetic mutator identities aren't all they're cracked up to be. How can I put it? When I get, uh, agitated, the disguise tends to break up."

Intrigued, I peer closely at her head. "So, it's not really human hair?"

"Certainly not!" says Catfish, appalled at the suggestion. "This is the finest microfibre blend from Asthenia. Each fibre was meticulously created between moonrise and moonset by a juvenile arachnigig following hours spent contemplating the teachings of the Great Asthenian Orb Weaver."

"Well, let's see if we can calm you down with a nice cup of tea."

Sipping at her tea, Catfish hums quietly to herself and then proceeds to tell me her mission. "I assume your grandmother told you about our revered leader, polkingbeal67?"

"Uh, yes, indirectly. My dad told me."

"Polkingbeal67 and your grandmother swapped hearts so that she could return to Earth."

"Yes, I know."

Catfish leans forward. "He wants it back."

"Erm, okay, well, I don't know if you realise this, but my grandmother passed away thirteen years ago."

"Hmm," is all she says.

"She lived a full and happy life. Sorry, Cat, we don't, uh, live as long as you people do. And what was that about him wanting his heart back?"

"Polkingbeal67 is our revered leader," says Catfish in a self-absorbed, mechanical monotone. Clearly upset and agitated, she slides off the chair and starts pacing up and down. I guess she's struggling to take in the news. But, hey, I'm wrong. "Neil, I was aware your grandmother might have died. We know you earthlings have a short lifespan."

I pull her hand away before it reaches her head and ask, "But something's upsetting you. What is it?"

"I'm upset about what I have to tell you next," she says. She sniffs as her face contorts, while her lips twitch and her nose starts to run. "Also, I'm sorry to hear about your grandmother. I knew her very well."

"I know," I tell her, sympathetically. "My dad told me she, uh, mentioned you."

Catfish nods and blows her nose on one of my tunics. "I hope you don't mind me telling you this, but she kissed me once."

"Oh yes, my dad told me – you were a penguin at the time."

"Yes, but I…" Catfish sniffs slightly squeakily, like your hamster does when you put your hand in the cage and it thinks it might be food. Wait though, your hamster might be sick – I'd get it checked out by a vet if I was you. Catfish turns her tear-stained face towards me. "I think she had a bit of a soft spot for me. You see, I rescued her at the celebrated nefeschaya incident. Also, I'm sure she will have mentioned enjoying my herky-jerky turkey dance? Shall I show you it?"

"No," I insist, "you're okay."

A flicker of disappointment flashes across her face. "Go on, tell me, what did your grandmother say about me?"

"Honest truth?"

"Honest truth."

"I believe you're the one she described as the narcissistic lunatic."

Catfish smiles. "Aww. Really? She thought I was the nicest lunatic? It is spoken. I told you she had a soft spot for me. What's a lunatic? Is it a moon-dweller? No! Did she think she was on the moon the whole time she was on our planet? No! Seriously?"

My thoughts are turning to lunch. Clearly, it's going to be a while before I can get Catfish back on track anyway. "I'm making turkey escalopes. Is that okay?" Placing a large piece of cling film over the turkey breast, I start slowly pounding it with a rolling pin.

Catfish looks thoroughly astounded. "You know that's not going to work, right? Are you trying to extract a confession? By the way, are you sure you don't want to see my herky-jerky turkey dance? Neil, come on, it's already dead."

"You're gonna hurt yourself putting thoughts like that together," I advise her. "Listen, why don't you, um…" The temptation to involve her in the preparation of lunch arrives like the Road Runner and disappears like Wile E. Coyote hurtling off the edge of a canyon. "No, it's okay, you can think about a fancy dress costume for tonight."

"A fisherman," Catfish replies in an instant. "I want to be a fisherman."

"You're a woman," I remind her.

"Does that mean I can't go as a fisherman?"

I concede that there's actually no reason why she can't go as a fisherman. And then I try to wind back the conversation to pick up the bit about her mission. "We'll sort out some stuff for you to wear later. Right after lunch. Now, what about polkingbeal67 and that thing you said - you know, about wanting his heart back?"

"So, let me explain," says Catfish, using apples from the fruit basket as a visual aid to facilitate her explanation. "Okay, well, your grandmother and polkingbeal67 swapped hearts so that she could return to the Pale Blue Dot. Sorry, you call it Earth." She moves two apples onto the table and then theatrically switches them over. "Then he and I had a bit of a mishap on the planet Oov – we kind of destroyed a chillok city. Total accident. Could have happened to anyone. So, long story short, we escaped to Earth." One of the apples is placed in an empty bowl. "Wait," she says, "I need to make it clear that this is the inferior earthling heart." She grabs a potato masher from the utensil rack and starts prodding, pressing and pummeling the apple.

"Excuse me!" I object. "That's my grandmother's heart you're grinding to pulp!" I remember my dad explaining this bit of the story over and over. I still don't really understand it. "So, why did you both come here, knowing full well his heart couldn't function?"

"Oh, it functioned for a while." She lets her voice tail off rather wistfully for a moment. "But it soon deteriorated." Sensing how baffled I am, she explains, "We, uh, forgot about the not functioning thing." Not much of an explanation, but hey. "Also," she goes on, "about the inferior heart thing – don't take it personally. I'm afraid it's what you get when your species has evolved from decomposing fungi like Tortotubus."

"Sorry, torto… what now?"

"Tortotubus. Yes, you see, about four hundred and forty million of your earth years ago, fungi began the rotting process which created layers of fertile soil, enabling plants to grow that would support animal life, which eventually led to you earthling humans arriving. You don't mind me pointing it out, do you?"

"No, no," I assure her, "it's great to know I'm basically descended from a pile of rotting fungus. Really."

She continues. "Anyway, then smolin9 comes along and he and polkingbeal67 swap bodies. Wait, what about *my* heart?" Another two apples are placed in the bowl. "Tch! I forgot *my* heart! No, that's no good. We'll get the apples mixed up. I'll use a banana."

"So you're the banana?"

"Yes."

"That figures," I murmur under my breath.

"So smolin9 acquires the bad apple, er, heart, and dies." Stifling a sob, she carefully tips the bad apple into the kitchen bin and pauses for a moment, tears welling up in her eyes. "Sorry 'bout that. Where was I? Ah, yes. Polkingbeal67, in smolin9's body, and I, in mine, return to Morys Minor, as it was called then. He now has the good apple, but it's not *his*. Your grandmother still has that one." She takes the apple and the banana out of the bowl and returns them to the fruit basket. Apples and bananas are transferred from basket to bowl and back again with bewildering rapidity as Catfish runs through a synopsis of further trips between the two planets. "Are you following me so far?"

"Oh yes," I confirm, valiantly trying to suppress another eye roll. "Crystal clear."

"Well, seeing as Mortian cardiac cells are far superior to your earthling ones, polkingbeal67's heart will have survived your grandmother's death and entered a state of suspended animation. And, yeh, he wants it back."

"But why?" I ask. "What's wrong with the heart he's already got? Smolin9's heart."

"I know what you're thinking," she says, fiddling aimlessly with the fruit in the bowl.

"You do?"

"You're thinking that makes no sense," she says, racking her brain for even the slightest glimmer of elucidation. Apparently, the challenge is way beyond her. "Well I suppose it, er, doesn't." Blathering away in an obvious attempt to draw attention away from the lack of logic, she continues in a rapid-fire stream-of-consciousness explanation. "The fact is, he wants it back and he told me to fetch it. Well, what can I do? He's the revered leader of our planet. I mean, put yourself in my shoes. I think it always helps to do that, don't you? But, no, you're a man and I'm a woman. I expect your feet are too big to fit in my shoes. Besides, a trip to Earth is always on everyone's 'to-do list' and I know I've been here before, but… "

I can't help wondering how long she can keep this up, but I put her out of her misery and interrupt her. "You might want to stop talking," I suggest.

Undeterred, Catfish rattles on, barely stopping for breath. "People say they can't tell if my glass is half-full or half-empty. Well, it is. I mean I never try to outrun my shadow and always try to look on the bright side and I figured there was a good chance I could get my hat back at the same time. Smash two glasses with one stone…"

"Shut up!" I insist, realising that communication with extraterrestrials is no different to talking with your own kind - occasionally, you simply have to tell someone to be quiet.

"Sorry," she says, "but this is so difficult. I mean how do you tell someone they've got to dig up their grandmother's body so that…"

"What?" I exclaim so loudly that a fish in my tropical aquarium does a somersault. If this was a cartoon, I think my jaw would have hit the floor. "There's no way you can…"

Catfish catches hold of my arms. "I knew this would come as a shock. The thing is…"

"No," I say, "you can't do that. And I mean you *can't* do that!" Fixing her with a look of profound anxiety, I speak as softly and slowly as I can manage. "She was cremated."

The look of horror on Catfish's face only deepens

when I pick up the bowl of fruit, tip it into the blender and proceed to make a tasty smoothie.

FISH OUT OF WATER

Disney is lingering at the bar, dressed as a witch. She's in her mid-forties, part Japanese, dyed platinum blond hair, cigarette lingering between her lips, a gleam of righteous zealotry lingering in her eyes. "Nice to meet you," she says to Catfish, who has just hopped up on the next stool and flashed a bright, slightly vacant smile from under the brim of her yellow sou'wester. "I'm Disney," she purrs, raising her cocktail glass with a sophisticated air of nonchalance. She oozes the accommodating and unconfrontational charm that is so characteristic of Japanese culture. "Hey, that's so cool! I just lurve your outfit!" Her eyes suggest otherwise as she scans Catfish's cable-knit crew neck sweater and marine boots with an expression of well-disguised distaste, as if she's politely declining to react to someone breaking wind. "Very creative! I think you and I are probably kindred spirits. I don't know about you, but I find my creative expression allows me to expand beyond my human existence and all the goings on in the world and remain awakened and vibrant and true to my divine human self."

"Oh, yes," says Catfish, nodding enthusiastically.

"Sometimes I get in a kind of zone where I can just turn my face to the sky and enjoy the photon energy pouring into the world. And I can feel so passionately alive!"

Her words take on an ethereal, hallucinatory quality and Catfish seems happy to walk into Disney's world of fluffy, dream-like speech bubbles. Beneath the ill-fitting sou'wester, her mouth is set in a fixed smile of exaggerated and incongruous politeness as she nods in tacit and probably fake understanding.

Disney's syrupy drawl is at odds with the burning intensity in her eyes. "I like to take opportunities such as this party to expand into new experiences of timelessness and I try to travel beyond the limitations of my mind and my physical reality and find harmony and freedom. And I just lurve to share it. I'm the sort of person who's very open with their magic. Have you seen my tattoos?" Pulling up her sleeves and lifting her top slightly to reveal swirling green and blue spirals, she laps up Catfish's evident approval. "*You* got anything interesting?"

Catfish nods and her eyes light up. Turning her back to me, she scoops up the hem of her sweater and out pops a perfectly limp Candy Basslet, one of the most colourful of all marine fishes and one which cost me a considerable proportion of my savings last year.

I don't know who is more shocked at this moment – Disney, who shrieks, drops her cigarette, spills her cocktail over her witch costume and disappears, or me, contemplating the demise of my beloved fish.

I assume Disney has taken refuge in the ladies' room – she's legged it out of here so fast, I'm surprised there isn't a Disney-shaped hole in the wall.

Catfish hasn't finished. Digging deep in her pocket, she produces a guppy and I can do nothing but stare at her in resigned consternation.

"According to my microwocky, it's a guppy," she announces as if she's unveiling Tutankhamun's tomb.

"Yes, I know. But shh, don't tell him. He thinks he's a Polka Dot Stingray," Staring forlornly at the hapless fish, I add, "Also, don't tell him he's dead."

Right now I don't have the time to remonstrate with Catfish. Outside, the blood moon is rising like a big ripe fruit above wisps of light clouds. Everyone's started drinking and talking and the party is getting into full swing. It's time to add some music and get the RECONNECT all-nighter underway.

My hands fly around the console, immersing the bar room in a neon blue glow. Some people immediately run to the dance floor as I unleash the opening bars of the remake of 'Do I Love You? (Indeed I Do).' Personally, I always find the intro pretty much stops me dead in my tracks. I'm too much in awe of the music to dance – it brings out goosebumps on my neck and I just want to listen to it. As I reorganise the pending track list, I keep one eye trained on the back of the bar room where Aysha is in earnest conversation with a few of her friends. Hair flowing down her back in auburn spirals, she self-consciously smooths her dress down over her knees and looks up for a second or two, allowing me the chance to establish eye contact. I smile and wave but stop short of signaling her to come over, even though that's exactly what I want to do. I'm finding it difficult to focus now. On anything. I guess there comes a point when you know that what you feel for someone has moved from friendship to something else. To what? I don't know, maybe infatuation, maybe romantic love.

Okay, not exactly the endorphin rush of love at first sight – more like the weathering process that produced the Statue of Liberty's green patina. No, that's not fair; that's a disservice. If it's like the Statue of Liberty, then it's the Statue of Liberty with *two* torches! Two torches held high! Anyway, I'm now as sure as I can be that I've crossed a threshold and the more I try to conceal it, the more it becomes a thing. But what do I say? And how do I say it? I don't want to come across as insincere. Or creepy or, let's face it, downright ridiculous. Caught up in the relentless groove of Frankie and the Classicals' 'What Shall I Do?', an exquisite remastered version with pitch changes in the chorus, I resolve to tell Aysha exactly what's going on with me. And I'll say it with no expectations of a response. I'll just say what I feel, and if she feels the same way, well, she can let me know in her own way and in her own time.

Plucking up my courage, I leave the console in auto mode and cross the room. I want this to be a moment we'll both always remember. Aysha and her friends are engaging in quite loud banter, not in a particularly offensive way, but enough to make me nervous and more than a little self-conscious. Nevertheless, I touch her on the arm. "Hey, Aysha."

"Oh, hey," she says.

"Um. Can I speak to you for a moment?" Every time I get close to her these days, I feel higher than a lark in the summer sky. No. Higher than a balloon dog in the summer sky.

We walk over towards the double doors which lead out to the garden. I don't know what's cooking out there, but the smell of food wafts over to us, spicy and rich. She smiles and, for a moment, I feel like there's just the two of us on the planet. "Remember when we were growing up," I begin, "everyone told us never to judge a book by its cover, yeah? They encouraged us to get to know people properly and to not go by first impressions. But of course we didn't listen and just made friends based on whether or not someone played Crazy Worm with us on the palmpad. Or whatever. If someone pushed past us in the lunch queue, we never forgave them. Either way, whatever we initially thought about someone, it kind of stuck. Remember?"

Aysha arches her eyebrows in a 'what on earth do you want?' sort of way. "Neil," she says, "did I refuse to play Crazy Worm wiv you when we were kids?"

"Er, no."

"Did I push past you in the lunch queue?"

"No."

She shrugs and throws her palms up in exasperation. "So, what the 'ell?"

"Well," I continue, losing confidence like a punctured hot air balloon. "As you get older, you come to realise that you change and other people change and you kind of have to adjust how you feel towards people. Don't get me wrong, sometimes your first instincts can be exactly right…" The words dry up. What the hell is going on? What happened to just telling her how I feel about her? So much for being honest and direct. So much for being prepared to take a chance.

Maybe it's fortuitous. Maybe it isn't. But Catfish, wearing an expression of abject misery, chooses this moment to come up and present me with my dead basslet.

"I've come to face the music," she says in a distraught tone. "I thought this fish would appreciate getting a different perspective on life. I've always felt sorry for fish. Spending their lives totally unaware of the world outside water. They don't know, do they?"

"Don't know what?" I ask.

"They don't know they're in water. Because they don't know anything else. To them, water is what the universe consists of. Just water."

While Aysha gapes in disbelief, I take the fish and place it gently in an ashtray containing three or four cigarette stubs. "You killed my fish," I point out, somewhat superfluously. "And you gave Disney the fright of her life."

"Hmm, yes," says Catfish, "Where is she? I never got the chance to ask her about balloon dogs. Can you help me find her?"

It's dawning on me that I really shouldn't leave Catfish to wander off alone. She looks a little unhinged and, frankly, I'm worried about what havoc she might wreak. "Sorry, Aysha, I'll catch up with you later?"

Aysha nods and rejoins her friends, who are now enjoying the night air. As Catfish and I return to the bar, we weave in and out of people dancing to the Yvonne Baker song, 'You Didn't Say A Word'. I love the song, but, right now, it kind of torments me. Quite honestly though, I'm going to have to worry about Aysha later. I'm more concerned about Catfish for the moment. Distracted and pale, she's lost her sou'wester and she's flapping irritably at long cables of hair that have worked loose from her casual topknot and fallen across her face. Her eyes are wide and she's breathing heavily as she speaks: "Where is she? Can you see her?"

"What's the hurry, Cat?" I ask. "Are balloon dogs really *that* urgent?"

"Between you and me, it's not about balloon dogs at all," she confides. "I just didn't want to alarm people."

"Alarm them? What do you mean?"

Catfish squints grimly at me and seizes the fur-covered sleeve of my werewolf costume. "I've been looking stuff up on my microwocky."

"And?"

"And, well, she's part-Japanese, yes?"

I nod my head and suggest we go outside. The music is too loud for a proper conversation.

As we sit at a small circular table, the light breeze lifts the damp hair at her temples but does nothing to cool her anxiety. Producing an aerosol of hair lacquer, she empties the can all over her head and proceeds to create random dramatic spikes pointing in all different directions. "Right," she says, conspiratorially. "Part-Japanese. Well, there's a Shinto legend about a sun goddess called Amaterasu and a moon god known as Tsukuyomi. They were brother and sister. According to ancient lore, Amaterasu sent Tsukuyomi to represent her at a feast presented by Uke Mochi, the goddess of food." Spotting what is presumably a look of vacant, uncomprehending bewilderment plastered across my face, she pauses for a moment and pulls at my sleeve once more. "Are you really focused on this?" she asks.

"Oh, uh, like a laser beam," I assure her.

She shoots me a cynical glance and carries on. "So, yes, the goddess, Uke Mochi, produced the food by turning to the ocean and spitting out a fish. Although it looked perfectly exquisite, Tsukuyomi was a bit miffed that the meal had been made in what he thought was a disgusting manner."

"And?"

"So he killed her."

I'm none the wiser. "And?"

"She's going to kill me!"

"Who is?"

"Disney, of course!"

"What?" For the life of me, I just cannot make the connection. Any connection. At all. "You realise Disney is not particularly enamoured with her Japanese heredity and actually tries to hide it? That's why she's dyed her hair and everything."

"Yes," says Catfish, ominously, "but *why* is she trying to hide it?"

I can't think of a suitable response, so I stare at her, eyes wide, mouth agape. I realise this would be a great moment to end the chapter, but art isn't always in synch with real life and Catfish has more to say.

"You clearly haven't done the research that *I've* done," she says. Her tone is almost one of admonishment. "The studies we've carried out on you earthlings have shown that people can be disposed to murder others if they're suffering from a chemical imbalance in the hypothalamus part of their brains."

It's very uncharitable and I'm a bit ashamed of it really, but the thought comes into my mind that for Disney's 'balance' to be disrupted, this presupposes that she actually had a 'balance' to begin with. But I say nothing.

"Anything can trigger that imbalance," Catfish goes on. "In relatively primitive species, such as yours, all these things - folklore, traditions, mythology and customs - form a cultural heritage that can act as a motivational factor influencing all aspects of your behaviour. I've done the research. You have to do the research. It is spoken."

"Says the person who didn't suss out that a fish can't live without water," I say sardonically. "Besides, if we're so inferior and primitive, if we're so far below you on the evolutionary scale, why are you still hanging around? I mean, you can't fulfil your mission, because my grandmother was cremated. So what's keeping you here?"

"I haven't told you my mission," says Catfish. "Well, not all of it anyway."

"There's more?"

Out of the corner of my eye, I notice Aysha approaching very slowly, carrying something carefully in both hands in front of her. "I'm just guessin', of course," she says, directing her remark to Catfish, "but I fink this might 'ave somefin' to do wiv you?"

The object in question is Catfish's yellow sou'wester, filled nearly to the brim with water. Closer inspection reveals a selection of fish from my tank – a peacock gudgeon, two or three black neon tetras, a few panda corys and an angelfish. Mercifully, they look healthy enough, if a little lethargic.

A few of Aysha's friends and a rather inebriated Gene Taylor join us at the table.

"What the hell?" Taylor gasps between heavy breaths. "There are fish in there! What's happening?"

Aysha gazes at the sou'wester. "I found it jus' like that, propped up wiv towels in a basin in the ladies' loo."

"I didn't want them to miss the party," Catfish explains. "I tried to carry the tank but it was too heavy." Looking stressed and sheepish, she takes a cigarette from a pack Taylor has tossed onto the table and raises it to her lips.

Various people take it in turns to hold and admire the makeshift fish bowl before returning it to Aysha. Then Taylor offers Catfish a light and the unthinkable happens. As he staggers forward slightly, the lighter catches a stray spike of heavily lacquered hair. With a soft 'whoomph!' like a gas burner igniting in slow motion, Catfish's hair is obliterated in a column of flames. Cue a chorus of screams, shouts of alarm and general mayhem as everyone panics. Everyone, that is, except Aysha, who has the presence of mind to dump the contents of the sou'wester over Catfish's head.

Remarkably, with prompt assistance from everyone around the table, I manage to save all the fish apart from the angelfish and one of the neon tetras that seems to have disappeared completely.

With apposite timing, Ramsey Lewis's rousing rendition of 'Wade In The Water' blasts out of the speakers while a wretched-looking Catfish sits in splendid saturation, wiping soaked strands of hair out of her dripping face.

THIS LOVE-STARVED HEART OF MINE

When I return from supervising the rehabilitation of my fish in the tank in my apartment, I check the decks and crack my head on the speaker unit above the console. I wince, grab my glass and find Catfish still sitting at the table, looking a little disconsolate, a towel wrapped around her neck, while Taylor and a couple of Aysha's friends do their best to comfort her.

"So," says Taylor, his voice full of boozy, fake solicitous concern, "Are you sure you're okay now, sweetie?"

"I'm okay, thank you. A bit singed and a bit drenched. Wait, did you call me sweaty? I know I'm new round here but isn't that a violation of, er, something?" Catfish has clearly taken a dislike to Taylor since the finance conference.

"I said sweaty, er, sweetie, not sweaty," Taylor slurs, raising his glass and putting it back down again.

"Well, actually, that's patronising, demeaning and presumptive," snaps one of Aysha's friends.

"Oh no, please," says Taylor with a bitter sigh. "Don't get started on any feminist speeches! You women need to develop more of a thick skin. Listen, I faced ageism, sexism and, uh, Islamophobia, whatever, to get where I am." I'm not sure if he's joking, but coming from a straight white male atheist in his mid-thirties, it's certainly a bit of an odd statement to make.

"Women just want to be treated like human beings the same as you," Aysha's friend points out with as much patience as she can muster.

Once again, Taylor raises his glass and puts it back down. "Yeah, there it is – a gender agenda! Well, you know what? Wanting your gender to be treated as human beings is ridicule, er, radicule politics as far as I'm concerned. It's about replacing oppressive patriarchy with oppressive matriarchy. Yeah, it's like… it's like invading Poland. Hey, Vincent Churchill said that."

Aysha's friend clearly thinks about just bottling it up and walking away, but she can't help saying: "*Vincent* Churchill?"

"It was either him or the old Manchester United boss, Vincent Van Gogh," declares Taylor.

Anyway, I leave them to their argument and ask Aysha if she'd like to dance.

Well, that was brave. Really, I've absolutely no idea where it came from. I was just standing there totally transfixed by the sounds emanating from the bar: clinking glasses, loud voices, but, above all, the music. The way the upbeat melodies and surging choruses contrast with the sad, sad lyrics. It's such an exquisite paradoxical aesthetic. And for a moment I'm just kind of right inside the music, living every word, loving the sensations the songs create in my mind. Tears threaten to fill my eyes with the sheer beauty of what I'm hearing. It's almost like it's not of this world. And yet it's in the song of birds during a dawn chorus, it's in the wind breathing through slender reeds and meadow grasses, in the chirping of crickets in the noon-time heat, the moaning of trees in entangled tumult during a tropical storm, the conspiratorial whispering of hidden streams and the sorrowful crashing of waves against the sand. Remember I collided with the speaker unit earlier? Well, clearly, that was quite a bang on the head.

'This Love Starved Heart Of Mine' starts up, the hairs on the back of my neck start to tingle, an emotional impulse strikes deep into my soul and the words just come out: "Hey Aysha. Wanna dance?"

"I dunno," she drawls, eyeing me critically. "Maybe you should dance wiv your new friend. I fink you've got a lot more in common wiv 'er. You can talk about fish an' stuff."

Oh no. What's happening? This is some sort of jealousy thing surfacing here, isn't it? The fear of losing something you have? But what does Aysha think she has that is now being jeopardised? Does this animosity towards Catfish mask feelings of insecurity? But why? What could possibly be underlying her mistrust? Why would she feel threatened by Cat's oddball persona, her apparent eccentricity, whatever? Or is it not about Cat at all? Perhaps it's about me. The truth is, I'm not really familiar with the anatomy of female jealousy. I have no idea if I should be encouraged or discouraged. In fact, I have absolutely no idea how to play this. At all. There again, perhaps Aysha's just making a few throwaway remarks and I'm overthinking things as usual. Thinking is great for fixing problems, but *overthinking* can be like solving problems that aren't even there yet – you just conjure them up in order to exercise your prowess at resolving them.

"Cat and I have only just met," I protest. "We don't have *anything* much in common."

Why do I have to have such a loud voice? Catfish hears me even over the music and all the background noise and chatter. "Yeah," she says in a seen-it-all tone she's probably picked up from listening to Disney. "We just sleep together."

The buzz of voices stops abruptly like someone shoving a stick in the spokes of a wheel. When she speaks again, it's like her voice is magnified a hundred times and her words seem to echo around the walls of a cavern. "And I fix him breakfast and cut his toenails. That's all." With that, she heads off to join people on the dance floor.

I cannot even begin to describe the look that comes over Aysha's face. Mere words cannot possibly convey the degree of hurt, disappointment and bitterness etched upon it. I feel terrible myself. I mean, what if she finds out Catfish also braided my hair last night? Listen, it's not my fault – I thought she was checking for nits. Sometimes things happen that inflict emotional wounds so deep you can almost feel physical pain. Fact is, a knife has been plunged, the very survival of our friendship is compromised and we're in a scenario where CPR must be performed immediately. I get up from the table and motion to Aysha to follow me. She ignores me. My mind's circuitry begins to fry and I feel beads of perspiration forming on my forehead.

Desperate to find something to divert attention from the tension, I conveniently notice something in Taylor's beer. "Look," I point. "Is that a bit of a pretzel or something floating in your beer?" It isn't. It's the missing black neon tetra fish.

Taylor pushes his glass away with an expression of disgust and wanders off to join the others watching Catfish doing her herky-jerky turkey dance, wet spiky tendrils of brown hair flailing around her head.

I'm barely aware of it, but that just leaves me and Aysha sitting at the table. No, that's a lie – I'm *acutely* aware of it. So, what shall I say? Judging by the look on her face, I'm pretty sure if I try to explain all the garbage Cat came out with, Aysha will just leave. Maybe the only way to go is straight through the middle. Nothing circuitous. Just cut all the crap, tell her how I feel about her and take it from there. Before I have the chance to say anything at all, however, she gets up and strides away into the garden.

Following her, I speak her name, but she keeps walking, the distance between us small at first, but increasing with each step. "Aysha!" I call. "Aysha, listen to me. I need to talk to you."

She stops without turning round.

I don't have any experience at this sort of thing, but what would it have taught me if I had? To hang on to hope whilst not trusting too much in it either? Does that make sense? Hmm, I've got a bad feeling about this, but I guess I just trust people with my heart, even when I suspect it'll get broken. "Aysha," I continue, "I'm going to tell you straight out. I think I'm falling…"

"No!" she shouts, finally turning around to face me. "No, don't! Jus' don't tell me you're fallin' in love wiv 'er! Really? After all we've been through togevver on this project? I thought I knew you. But maybe not. Maybe I was wrong. Maybe I don't know you *at all*. You know what? I thought we was like unbreakable chains that couldn't be broken. I 'ave to tell you, Neil, I feel sooo let down. I trusted your judgement. I looked up to you." For just a split second, there's an opportunity for me to cut in, but I miss it. She goes on, scarcely taking a breath: "Tell me, is it a pity thing? Is she ill? Is she gonna die of cancer or somefin' and you're not tellin' us? Did you commit a crime togevver?… Feel free to stop me any time you like. I'll need to go to the bathroom soon... Perhaps you're in danger? P'rhaps it's part of a Russian plot to infiltrate our scientific institutions. Or is it the Chinese? Are you bein' 'eld against your will? Blink twice for yes. Are the fish bugged? Do you want us to call the police? Blink twice!"

I now have no choice. I have to tell not just one truth, but all the truths I have. "Catfish is an extraterrestrial." As soon as the words leave my lips, I want to snatch them back. I cannot believe how lame that sounds.

Nor can Aysha. "Yeh," she snaps, "because that's much more plausible than *anythin'* I just came up wiv. How dare you!" She stops short of slapping me, but nothing short of an earthquake can stop her diatribe now. "I really thought you were better than this," she snarls in a voice that sounds like someone scraping burnt toast. "But you're just like all the others. One bat of those foot-long eyelashes and you're gone. Y'know what? I don't care. I don't give a damn. It's your life. Do what you want." Flicking her hand dismissively, she turns her back on me and walks away, leaving me to stagger around blindly in my bleak and barren world of bewilderment and things left unsaid. So it turns out that hope is cold-blooded. It has no conscience at all. No conscience, no remorse, no soul. I don't know the word for what it is I'm feeling, but it's powerful. It grabs you, hurls you around and leaves you howling at the blood moon like a wild dog.

I'm not sure what's happening at this moment. Oh yes, I must be wandering aimlessly back to the music console, because that's where my feet seem to be taking me. According to scientists, the brain has highly specialised structures for music. At times like this though, the sophisticated parts of your brain are the first things to shut down – I have no idea what songs are playing. I can't focus on anything. Apart from a few brief flickers of brain activity that flare angrily every so often, I just sink into a velvety black melancholy.

I've always believed certain people, destined to be together, possess a parapsychological connection, a mystic bond, if you like, that cannot be sundered by boundaries, barriers, distances or misunderstandings. I've always believed these attachments have roots so deep that other people's storms can only bend them and never knock them over. Yep, I've always believed that. Well, now I don't. Or, at least, If I still believe it, I'm sure Aysha and I don't have such a bond.

LAMBDA

Some of the dancers are fairly good. Most of them settle for basic side-to-side steps and arm shimmies in time with the beat, but others really tear it up on the choruses – fast spins and flips and back drops. It's quite exhilarating, especially with so many people in fancy dress costumes. I'm flicking through my playlist, trying to find songs that fit my mood when Disney shows up. "Have you seen my hat?" she asks. Well, obviously that question reverberates a bit. It reverberates like the drums of my wretched fate. "My witch hat," she adds.

"Your what hat?" I ask.

"My witch hat."

"No need to be pedantic. Which, what, whatever."

"No, I mean my witch's hat. The black pointy one I was wearing earlier."

"Disney, do you believe in fate? Do you believe things happen for a reason and you don't get to choose?"

"You mean losing my hat might be part of the grand scheme of things?" Her laughter is like pebbles rolling down a corrugated roof. I note that she appreciates her own jokes just a little too enthusiastically. "I'm sorry," she says. "I think fate is something we're born with. As we get older, we get more control over it. Does the crow of the cockerel cause the sun to rise? No. Does this slider make the music louder? Yes. There are causes and effects. Causes sometimes result in effects and effects sometimes have causes, but sometimes there are just accidents. Sometimes two things may happen at roughly the same time, but if that's evidence for causation, it's just circumstantial."

Seriously, I've absolutely no idea what she's talking about and I tell her so.

"Well, anyway," she says, shrugging. "I guess you just have to play the cards that life deals you."

"Yeah, well, I'm pretty sure the deck in this game is missing some cards," I reply sardonically. "Tell me something. If you have feelings for someone, do you think you should let them know?"

Disney passes me my glass. "Drink up," she tells me. "I'll tell you what I think. You shouldn't deny or ignore your feelings. Let them exist by all means, but don't let them drive your actions. You don't have to buy into them. Feelings are ambiguous anyway. They can encourage you to open doors within you that have 'No entry' written on them. And that may or may not be a good thing. Sometimes doors have 'No entry' on them for very good reason."

"In my case, the door just slammed in my face," I mutter. "And I think it's closed for good. It's so closed, it's not a door any more. It's become part of the wall."

Catfish joins us. She's swapped her sou'wester for a balloon hat. "Can you make a dog sculpture out of this hat?" she asks Disney, clearly no longer suspecting Hinton's sister of murderous intentions.

"I propose a quid pro quo," says Disney, adroitly pinching and twisting the balloons as she speaks. "I'll make you a dog if you help me find *my* hat."

"Where did you have it last?" Catfish asks, eyes glued to Disney's squeaky but skilful manipulation of the balloons.

The tip of Disney's tongue protrudes between her lips in concentration as she applies a twist lock. "Let me think," she intones slowly. "I had it when I went to the loo. Then I took it off to fix my hair. Ah, I think I left it at the side of the sink." She applies another twist lock and licks her top lip. "No, wait. I thought someone else might take it, so I picked it up and folded it and, er, put it in my, er, …"

Catfish produces the hat from Disney's handbag.

"Ah," says Disney, unfolding the hat and placing it on her head.

"I'm going to take the dog for a walk," says Catfish. "I think I'll call him Lambda."

I walk outside with her and ask her about her apparent fixation with balloon dogs. As we stroll towards the statue of Nicnevin, the soft moonlight filters through shadowy, diaphanous clouds, lending a mystical aura to the shimmering surface of the lake. The deep quiet of the night is occasionally disrupted by muted sounds from the woods in the distance.

"I've done some research," Catfish explains rather theatrically. "You have to do the research. It is spoken."

"Oh no, not again," I think to myself.

"According to my studies of earthling culture, dogs on your planet are symbols of protective powers and loyalty. Is that right?"

"I guess so."

"Our revered leader, my mentor, polkingbeal67, told me about a tribe of earthlings he was particularly impressed with."

"Really?" I ask with slightly exaggerated enthusiasm. To be fair, I've got other things on my mind.

"The Cheyenne. I hope that answers your question."

"Yeah, they became extinct a couple of hundred years ago."

Catfish's mouth drops in astonishment. "Oh no!" she exclaims.

"Well, actually," I explain, "That's not strictly accurate. I think a few thousand still live on reservations in America. But they're no longer the warrior people you're probably thinking of."

"What do they do now then?"

"Um, I expect they just kind of try... not to become extinct," I suggest.

"How disappointing," says Catfish. "Anyway, when they *were* warrior people, they considered dogs to be sacred because of their ferocity and toughness. They named their best warriors the Dog Soldiers and put them in charge of protecting and guarding their villages. Polkingbeal67 loves to tell stories about them."

Something my father told me about polkingbeal67 springs into my mind. "I heard that the first thing polkingbeal67 did when he came to Earth was shoot a dog."

Catfish's eyes widen as if she's just sat on something sharp. "Naturally," she blusters, her face reddening with embarrassment. "He thought he was being attacked."

"The dog was on a lead. In a park."

"As you said, it was his first visit to the planet. He didn't want to take any chances. Dogs can be very fierce. Listen, I refuse to apologise for our revered leader. I don't care what the facts are."

"Anyway," I continue, unable to suppress a smile, "if you want a dog for protection, why don't you get a *real* dog? I mean, I don't think *balloon* dogs are particularly fierce, do you?" To demonstrate the point, I attempt to provoke Lambda by poking him with my finger.

Catfish snatches the dog away. "Hey!" she exclaims, with a concerned look on her face.

"Okay, okay," I laugh. "I guess even balloon animals have rights?"

"Balloons are important to me."

I think I heard that right, but just to be sure, I say "Pardon?" I wish I hadn't.

Catfish delivers a lecture on the expanding nature of the universe using the analogy of dots on a balloon. "We learn this as infants on my planet," she says. "Balloons are important, Neil, as a means of explaining how the universe expands. Let me go through it again. The dots on the balloon represent galaxies. As the balloon inflates, the dots get further apart. From the point of view of each dot, all other galaxies are moving away. Verily."

I simply have to interrupt. "Sorry, Cat, but I'm already familiar with the analogy. We learn this in *our* schools. So, I guess we're not as primitive as you might think."

As we approach Nicnevin, the silent sentinel of the gardens, the pale underwings of an owl can be seen drifting across the lake. I fancy I can see its fiery, yellow eyes. High above us, but also reflected in the water stretching out to our right, a myriad of stars glint and shimmer like sparks frozen in time.

"Well," says Catfish, looking more than a little crestfallen, "I bet you can't explain *parallel* universes. I've been in one."

For some reason, I figure the best response to this is to poke Lambda once again.

On this planet, when people feel slighted or demeaned in some way, it's not uncommon for them to react in a dramatic fashion. Mortians, it appears, are just the same.

"I regret to inform you - your planet's being invaded!" cries Catfish with a flourish of her hand.

"It's just an owl," I assure her.

"No, not the owl," she says, dismissing my flippancy with an expression of urgent anxiety. "I'm serious. Look at me! Your entire planet is being invaded by chilloks and you don't have long to survive." She waits for this to sink in before continuing, "I told you there was another part of my mission here. This is it. I'm here to warn you of the danger you're in. You and all your people. You're going to be wiped out." She pauses once more. "It is spoken."

I'm fully aware that the chilloks might possibly have attempted something like this before, back in 2047, but the revelation still knocks me for six. It's difficult to know how to respond to news like this. "What the devil do you mean?" is the best I can manage for now.

"I don't know how else to put it," says Catfish. Holding Lambda out in front of her, she wrings his neck and makes a croaky sound with her throat. "All of you. Doomed. Finished. Done for. Kaput. Bereft of life. Put out of your misery. One foot in the grave. Pushing up daisies. Does that answer your question?"

"Yeh, yeh, okay," I cut in, "I get that. But how? Chilloks are just miniscule, insect-like creatures. How do they do it? Wait, you *are* serious, aren't you?"

Catfish nods in affirmation and says, "Yep."

"So how can we stop them?"

"The invasion is already in progress," says Catfish, chewing her bottom lip.

"If they're the same creatures that were responsible for the Nebraska swarms of 2047, we defeated them using gene warfare."

"Won't work with cerebrum ambulans."

Do I hear an eerie whispering? I suppose I half-expect to see the moon and stars obliterated by vast swarms of biting, blood-sucking winged insects, humming and buzzing and transforming the night sky into the seething, smouldering mouth of hell itself. But all I can see is an orange balloon that must have made a break for freedom through the double doors.

"Really? It's already happening?" I ask feebly. "How? I haven't seen any, y'know, swarms or whatever. What *sort* of invasion?"

Catfish takes my arm. "Do you need to sit down?" she asks helpfully. Actually, it's not all that helpful – there are no seats in the immediate vicinity. "How much do you know about the chilloks?"

I can only shake my head in agitation and exasperation.

Taking a deep breath, Catfish starts to unravel the mysteries of the queer alien creepy-crawlies I'd heard about from the account of my grandmother's extraterrestrial experiences. "Well, chilloks are divided into four castes, one of which, the cerebrum ambulans, invades humanoid skulls and interferes with brain function."

"Like a computer virus?"

"If you like. It's called braintuning. Anyway, these chillok microbe entities implant themselves in people's brains and kind of hypnotise them to do their bidding."

"Wait," I butt in, recalling something my dad told me. "I thought it didn't work with humans on Earth? My dad said it only works with Mortian brains."

Catfish nods slowly. "That used to be the case," she says. "But they've sorted that out now.

"Progress is a wonderful thing."

"It's no joke," Catfish remonstrates. "They infiltrated *my* brain before my exile in a parallel universe. It's a terrible experience. Of course, they didn't find it very easy. Apparently my brain was one of the greatest challenges they ever came across."

"Yeah, I can imagine."

"It's true," Catfish insists. "I was supposed to think of myself as a chillok."

"But you didn't?"

"No. I thought of myself as a penguin."

"Yes, well, I can see how that fooled them completely."

Picking up on my insincerity and eager to demonstrate her mental acuity, Catfish challenges me to come up with the toughest riddle I can possibly devise.

"Okay, well, what colour is my tunic?"

"That's not a riddle," she complains.

"Just bear with me," I say. "What colour is my tunic?"

"White," she answers, suspiciously.

"Correct. Now spell the word 'silk'."

"S-I-L-K."

"Excellent. Now tell me what cows drink."

Catfish is sucked in completely. "Milk," she says, looking quite pleased with herself.

"Yep," I smile. "No doubt about it. Your brain must have presented the chilloks with the greatest workout of their lives."

"Don't worry," says Catfish, completely guilelessly. "I'll give you some tips."

"Yeah, thanks. So, anyway, what does this invasion look like? How come I haven't noticed columns of ant-like creatures marching up people's necks and into their ears, waving banners and beating drums?"

"Oh," says Catfish, "you can't see them at all. They're microscopic. But have you heard people speaking Latin? That's usually a pretty good indication that a person's brain has been infiltrated."

I stare open-mouthed, then a tiny seed of realisation starts to germinate, pushing aside my cynicism and scorn. For some time now, Latin-themed game shows have become a staple on VR television. Songs with Latin lyrics have dominated the music charts. Latin phrases are dropped casually into everyday conversation at home, in the cruiser and on the streets. Not bad for a supposedly dead language. Now I think about it, certain people have become almost obsessive about using it. Certainly, Hinton springs to mind.

"Ah! I've just thought of something that will help explain it," says Catfish. "No, sorry, it's gone."

A cool breeze blows across the lake, producing the calming sound of lapping water. I sit on the ground, while Catfish leans against the side of the statue and resumes her disclosure. "It started centuries ago when the chilloks developed a taste for the sweet, sticky substance excreted by plant-sucking Mortian aphids. The cerebrum ambulans got into the aphids' heads and interfered with their photoreceptors, persuading them it was permanently day time, so that they wouldn't stop producing the honeydew the chilloks thrived on. The braintuning techniques they use are known as neutralisation and transposition. With neutralisation, thoughts that are potentially injurious to chillok sensibilities are snuffed out at the neuron level. Transposition involves replacing such thoughts with contradictory ones."

I have to say I'm finding it difficult to reconcile the knowledgeable analyst delivering this erudite clarification with the numbskull who can be persuaded so easily that cows drink milk. Then I look round the plinth and see she's reading from a strange orb-shaped minicomputer device. I assume that's her microwocky.

Voices and sounds from the bar are amplified by the water and it's as if the dark lake itself is laughing in a cold, hollow voice as a backdrop to Catfish's clipped, rapid phrasing. "The chillok worker caste contains neuroscientists who developed the concept that thoughts are energies, capable of existing independently of a creature's physical body and capable of being connected with another creature's consciousness – disembodied bubbles of intellect that float away freely to seek new hosts. These particular chilloks, working in tandem with the cerebrum ambulans have been largely responsible for the large-scale offensive directed against earthling humans."

Out of the corner of my eye, I notice her putting the device away in her bag. She looks at me expectantly, the way people do when they've asked a question and they're waiting for your answer. I say absolutely nothing. The moon reappears from behind a cloud and the soft illumination reflects off the water.

Catfish stifles an embarrassed cough.

I gather my thoughts and then scatter them all over the place. "But if they really *are* doing this braintuning thing, what's the point? What do they want us to think or do or say or believe? What are they seeking to gain by it? When you say they're going to wipe us out, what do you mean? How? How can they wipe us out by manipulating our thoughts?"

Still pale and motionless and dappled with imperfections, the moon, inspired perhaps by the proximity of the unwavering Polaris star, is now shining with growing self-confidence. Tonight, it seems it's trying to forget its dark side. "Well, it's not easy to explain," says Catfish, whose face is bathed in the ethereal light. "What they do is, they kind of lock people away in their own separate parallel universes. Their own little bubbles of loneliness, if you like."

"On the basis that we're stronger together, and weaker apart?"

"Yes," she confirms. "That's it. That's what they're doing."

This is beginning to make a bit of sense, I suppose. According to various surveys, loneliness has become alarmingly widespread in recent times, prompting experts to examine profound changes in the way we live and interact. Most of the reports I've read, for example, have expressed concern that technology is being used far too much as a replacement for real human interaction. But what if the truth lies elsewhere? Maybe, just maybe, we really *are* being bamboozled and hypnotised by these infernal brain-mashers. Then the full realisation dawns on me. "Oh, I get it," I say. "They make us depressed and we eventually take our own lives?"

Catfish nods. "That way, you'll eventually get wiped out completely and the Intergalactic Court of Justice, Arbitration and Conciliation won't suspect the chilloks at all. The perfect crime."

Wow. Sorry, but 'wow' is all I can manage at the moment.

Catfish coughs again. "Shall I get polkingbeal67 down here?" she suggests. "Maybe he can help explain it all better."

Shaking my head, I stare up at the moon. "No," I decide. "I don't think that will help at all. With one Mortian down here, what happens? I get no more fish. With *two* Mortians down here, I might get, I dunno, maybe twice as much no more fish."

As we make our way back towards the bar, I ask, "Aren't there, y'know, some intergalactic guardians of peace and justice who can intervene and save us from all this braintuning invasion malarkey?" For no particular reason, I give Lambda another poke.

"Don't worry. There *is* a solution," Catfish assures me. "They tried the same thing on our planet and were only defeated when polkingbeal67 delivered a masterpiece of oration in the Smolin9 Grand Hall. He spoke to them of friendship and reconciliation and the sanctity of life and pan-galactic respect and a whole load of drivel like that. And it worked."

"Wait, are you saying he just talked them out of it?"

"Well, not exactly. Apparently, it was all to do with brain chemicals."

"Neurotransmitters?" I suggest.

"Yes," Catfish confirms, raising her eyebrows in surprise. "You know about those? Dopamine, serotonin, oxytocin, endorphins and hartglue."

"Hartglue?"

Catfish nods vigorously like a bobble head doll. "That's the key molecule. That's the one that really did the trick for us."

"So, in order to defeat these brain-chewing chilloks, we just have to come up with a suitable cocktail of neurotransmitters? Like, produce an antidote composed of happy chemicals?"

"Hmm," says Catfish apologetically with a sheepish smile. "There's a snag."

"Of course," I groan. "There *has* to be a snag."

"The problem is, you earthlings don't produce anything like enough of these molecules any more. And they disappear almost as soon as they're created, because you've become almost completely deficient in hartglue."

"I don't think we've even discovered yet that we had it."

"That's possible," says Catfish. "And it's serious, because hartglue is the molecule that sustains the others."

"We're missing the key molecule."

"Yes."

"I might have known."

Setting Lambda on the ground beside her, she reaches into her bag, rummages around for a second or two and then triumphantly produces a small, cylindrical container. "Hartglue!" she announces with all the aplomb of a magician pulling a rabbit from a hat. "I brought some with me. I just need to work with one of your biochemist people, and ta-da!"

Well, that gets me energised. My eyes must be lighting up like Christmas and the Fourth of July rolled into one. "Well, yes," I enthuse. "That's definitely something to put at the top of your ta-da list! Why didn't you mention that straight away? We both know a biochemist!"

"We do?"

"Disney!" I shout eagerly. "Disney is a biochemist!"

"It is spoken!" declares Catfish. "We must call on her first thing in the morning."

"Well, I realise time is of the essence, but this is an all-nighter," I remind her. "Everyone'll be sleeping in the morning."

"The next day then," says Catfish. "No later."

She looks so pleased with herself, it seems a shame to point out that Lambda has blown away on a sudden gust of wind. Floating lazily through the air, the flying dog seems to acquire a life of its own, whirling, spinning and zigzagging around the garden as Catfish sets off in forlorn pursuit.

While she's gone, I mull over the outrageous events of the day, grapple with the implications and end up flattened by the sheer magnitude of it all. "That's just great," I think to myself. "First, I have serious friendship issues. And now it appears the entire planet is being threatened by brain-munching insects. I had a feeling today was going to be crap." But by the time Catfish reappears looking a little drained and disheveled, my mood has picked up somewhat. "Sit! Sit!" I say, addressing Lambda.

Bewildered and confused, Catfish drops to the ground and settles cross-legged on the lawn. I laugh all the way back to the bar. And then the enormity of Catfish's revelation threatens to overwhelm me once more. I should be okay. Recently, I've become a bit of an expert at managing stress through relaxation techniques such as deep breathing, meditation and mindfulness. Just kidding – I need another cocktail. And I need it now!

Rejoining the others around the table, I listen with detached interest since I'm in no mood to join in any conversation. The voices become distant, smaller. My head is spinning with the frightening ramifications of what I've just heard. Has my own brain been taken over? Latin phrases knock persistently at the door of my mind like Jehovah's Witnesses. At first, I pretend I'm not at home, but that doesn't stop them. Then I pretend I'm German, but then the cunning so-and-sos send a pair of German-speaking Witnesses round. Hang on, does that make sense? Latin phrases in German? I think I'm losing it. I force myself to refocus on the conversation at our table.

"I've had my hovercar repossessed by the bank," Taylor announces to no one in particular. He seems to be talking to his glass of beer. "And now, guess what? Double whammy. Now I've lost my flash car, my wife's decided to leave me. Can you believe that?"

"That's terrible, Gene," says one of Aysha's friends. "Terrible. Simply terrible. I hope you'll be okay."

Taylor scratches his beard. "Yeah, I'm really going to miss that car."

"You're an ass," snaps Aysha's friend, tossing the wig of her Cruella de Vil outfit.

"Yeah, well, Cruella, I might be an ass, but you're cruel. You're cruel to animals," says Taylor, woozily, motioning towards Lambda, "You'd better keep that dog away from this woman!"

Suddenly everything is moving in slow motion. Taylor performs a drunken impression of Cruella de Vil swishing a fur coat around and knocks the back of a floaty, sending the contents of Catfish's bag cascading onto the floor. Picking up the hairbrush phaser gun, he sticks the thin end of it in his mouth like a cigarette holder. Catfish and I stare in petrified disbelief and terror.

"He's got your, uh, hairbrush!" I hiss at Catfish out of the corner of my mouth and try to rise casually to my feet but my legs refuse.

"Do something!" Catfish hisses back.

Before either of us *can* do anything, Taylor grabs Lambda and stabs him with the bristles of the hairbrush. There's a loud pop. Catfish crumples to the floor in a dead faint. So, of course, does Lambda.

Taylor grins and belches. "In the world of balloon animals," he says, "the hedgehog is king!"

NEVER EXPLAIN ANYTHING

Sleeping on the sofa is not ideal. I might just as well have dozed away on an ironing board. Lack of proper rest makes me more emotional than usual and I feel quite upset. I've been messaging Aysha, but she still has her CC configured for automatic bounce-backs. When I woke up earlier this afternoon, I even slipped a paper note under her apartment door, basically asking if we're still friends. I haven't had a reply. They say that if you love someone you should let them go, but how does that make any sense? Okay, I'm being a bit disingenuous here. I know perfectly well it *does* makes sense. I know you have to ensure mutuality. I know you have to take that leap of faith and give the object of your affections total freedom to choose. Otherwise, you risk pouring a lot of time and effort into a relationship that's destined to fail. Nevertheless, I can't help wondering - what the hell do you do when you've let someone go and she doesn't come back?

I put the question to Catfish as she plays with the eggs on the kitchen unit. "Tell me, Cat - when it comes to a friendship, when should you fight for it and when should you let go?"

Scratching her head in puzzlement, she seeks clarification: "Is this person attached to you by rope?"

"What? No, why?"

"Then don't let go," she says in a decisive tone. "Wait, has this person got any carrots?"

"What?"

"I want to make a carrot omelette."

"*We've* got carrots. They're in the vegetable rack over there."

"Then it's okay to let go. We've got our own carrots."

Why did I expect Catfish to say anything remotely sensible? "Hmm," I say to myself. "Let go? I tell you what, it's damn hard to let go when you're being pushed off a cliff for no reason whatsoever."

Catfish turns to me with a superior grin. "That's why I asked about the rope!"

What the hell? Sometimes she says things that just leave me dumbfounded. I mean, what the hell? Sometimes she'll give me a surprisingly persuasive answer to a question I didn't ask or I'll feel I've lost an argument with her that I wasn't even making. Conversations with her are as predictable as the flight pattern of an inebriated wasp. I watch as she arranges the eggs on the unit and draws lipstick faces on them.

There's a knock on the door and Aysha walks in. Glancing towards Catfish, she says, "Uh-huh," and turns on her heels.

"No, wait, Aysha, please!" I say, grabbing her gently by the arm. "Please give me a chance to explain what this is all about. Please."

Pursing her lips, she cocks her head to one side and says, "Well, okay, I'm listenin'. An' I 'ope you've got somethin' better than 'Catfish is an extraterrestrial'!"

Catfish and I exchange glances and say nothing. A panicky feeling starts growing in my chest.

Aysha shakes her head. "Oh, you are kiddin' me!"

Turning to Catfish, I implore her as earnestly as I can, "Cat, tell her. Tell her everything you've told me. Please, please just explain it all."

"What, now?" Catfish asks. "Well, okay, he's right. He's quite correct. I'm an extraterrestrial. My name is yukawa3 and I'm from a planet known as Smolin9."

"Good," says Aysha, thumbing her chin, a sardonic smile playing on her lips. "Well, will you please take me to *your* planet? I don't like this one any more and I, uh, I don't wanna live in a world where Neil is right! When you two have quite finished takin' the mick out of me…"

"Seriously, hear this out," I urge her. "I'm sorry but you've just got to trust me. Please."

Aysha sits down and for the next two hours Catfish and I go through everything that's happened using the eggs with lipstick faces to illustrate the people involved. Before we even get to the stuff about happy chemicals and antidotes, Aysha's expression changes from open-mouthed incredulity to mere open-mouthed disbelief. Progress at last.

"Prove it!" Aysha challenges. "I mean, let's face it, you look like a regular human woman, uh, one of us, so why should I believe you're in some sort of disguise? And why on earth, ha ha, if you're so clever, did you choose a name like Catfish Tunic? No one on this planet is called Catfish. What were you thinkin'?"

"I didn't choose the name," Catfish explains.

I own up. "*I* chose the name."

Aysha rolls her eyes. "Yeh, that figures."

"I let him choose a name on my behind," says Catfish.

"I think you mean 'on your *behalf*.'"

"Anyway, she *likes* the name," I protest in a slightly injured tone. Well, hey, I think it was an inspired choice.

Twirling her hair in her fingertips, Catfish points out, "I wanted to be Mary Poppins. He wouldn't let me."

"Hmm," says Aysha, with a mischievous glint in her eyes. "Supercatfish'slipstickeggsarereallyjustatrocious!"

I laugh. "That's pretty good, Aysha." It wasn't.

She smiles and suddenly we time-warp back to happier times and spend a couple of minutes discussing favourite movies. "Anyway," she says, turning to Catfish, who has no idea what we're talking about. "Tell me somethin' that will persuade me that you're, uh, really an alien."

"Okay," says Catfish, relishing the challenge. "Have you seen my herky-jerky turkey dance?"

"No, uh, yes," says Aysha, curling her top lip. "What's that got to do with, uh, anythin'? Wait, actually I *did* see you dancin' – and, yeh, it *is* definitely quite alien. No, listen, I'm an X-ray astronomer. Tell me somethin' 'bout the universe. Tell me somethin' sciencey."

"Like what?"

"Well, I dunno. Surprise me. Listen, we, uh, earthlings kinda know everythin' in the universe is made up of fermions an' bosons. An' we know about antimatter counterparts. But is there somethin' else? What's the next thing we need to know to make wormhole travel an' stuff possible for us? If you're really from some advanced civilisation, why don' you tell me somethin' useful we *don't* know?"

Catfish crosses her legs, swings her foot and tries valiantly to look like she's considering a perspicacious answer. In fact, I'm pretty sure her mind is as blank as the gaze of one of the lipstick-face eggs. We earthlings may have mastered autonomous robotics, molecular nanotechnology and 3D printed food systems, but, quite honestly, I couldn't tell you how a magnet works or explain why it rains. Likewise, I suspect Catfish thinks elementary particles are the dreams that stuff is made of.

"I can pull my hair out!" she declares finally. And promptly does so. Clutching a significant clump of her own hazel-coloured hair, she grins at Aysha with smug satisfaction.

Aysha is not looking too impressed. I don't think I'd even describe it as grudging acknowledgement. But, frankly, I'm a bit surprised. Surely this should be an epiphany moment for her – it's not every day you see people yanking out handfuls of their own hair without even flinching. Aysha, however, merely shrugs and says, "Wait a minute. Uh huh. So you're askin' me to believe you're one of a species that has unlocked the secrets of intergalactic wormhole travel and, to demonstrate such incredible pioneerin' prowess, you're gonna pull out a bit of your hair? No, I tell you what, I'm not buyin' it. If you're an alien, turn yourself into your alien form! Now. Do it!"

With a look of alarm on her face, Catfish shakes her head and says, "I can't do that. Not right now. It takes over twenty-four hours of your earth time to do that. And then it'd be another twenty-four hours to resume my earthling identity. And I'd have to take HDA twice. Once to return to my normal form and then again to resume my disguise as Catfish. Plus, the after-effects are like having a hangover inside a tumble dryer."

"HDA?"

"Homeodynamic disruption antidote. It's horrible. Tastes like goopmutt droppings!" She tugs another strand of hair from her scalp.

"Please stop 'er doin' that," says Aysha. "I'm gonna 'ave to get 'er one of those neck cones people put on their dogs." Suddenly, her apparent cheerfulness vanishes like someone flipping a light switch. "Okay, listen, I think I've played along with your little game for long enough now. You're filmin' this, aren't you? Where's the camera? You just set this up to see how I'd react! Well, I 'ope you've 'ad your fun. I'm goin' now."

While I stare at the door that Aysha's just slammed behind her, Catfish tilts her head and examines me with her grey-flecked blue eyes. "Are you having an earthling emotion thing here? Are you going to cry a river of tears?"

"A what?" I ask. "Where did you get that from? No, I'm okay. Really."

If I *do* cry a river later, I guess I'll just walk to a bridge and get over it. Well, eventually. But for now I don't see how I can let go of someone I can't live without. The satnav navigating me through this part of my life is telling me to make a U-turn when possible, and, yep, I get it, I've lost my way.

But if I keep going, the satnav will adjust and figure out another route, won't it? Won't it?

LEARNING FROM GEESE

I think I slept relatively well last night. A glance at my CC and I realise it's gone eight o'clock already. No sign of Catfish up and about yet. Today's the day we simply must make some progress with the antidote. I pour a juice and knock on the bedroom door. Nothing. That's strange.

I call Aysha. Another bounce-back. To be honest, I'm not sure I'd know what to say to her anyway. Earlier, I mentioned feeling like a lark in the summer sky when I'm with her. Well, now I feel like my wings have been clipped and the view from here is taking on an entirely different aspect. Anyway, the other thing I must do is call Hinton. We exchanged comm-IDs at the bar during retro night and now I urgently need to get in touch with her sister. I settle back on the sofa as Hinton's face materialises on my CC.

We exchange polite greetings, she gives me Disney's comm-ID and then I make the mistake of engaging in conversation.

"It's nice to have the chance to chat to you," says Hinton, "Do you mind if I ask you something? Do you think I come across as a nice person?"

I nod, deciding that vague equivocation will suffice as a response to this.

"You'd say I have a secure and satisfying career, wouldn't you? By most people's standards, I have fulfilling relationships. I think I totally understand my value as a human being, as a professional and as a friend."

I nod again.

"Vir sapit qui pauca loquitur," says Hinton, smiling cryptically.

"What?" I ask. "Pardon?"

"That man is wise who talks little."

"Uh, yeah, sorry," I respond, trying not to appear too baffled.

"Listen, Neil, the truth is: I'm lying. It's all a sham. Nosce te ipsum. My job is a sham because the project is totally insular. External Relations? Apart from occasional conferences with WSC Treasury Department officials and the people working on the Euclid Space Agency mission, RECONNECT doesn't actually connect with the outside world *at all*. My best relationships are with the figurines on my living room mantle. I put hats on them and talk to them. All the rest of my friends are just profile pictures. I don't even like to spend a day with *myself*. That's why I take a lot of long naps during the day. So you see, my whole life is a sham. A lie. But, hey, it doesn't matter that it's a lie because no one listens anyway. Semper idem." A long, awkward silence descends before she speaks again. "Anyway, thank you so much for listening to all my problems, Neil. I appreciate it."

"Uh, oh yeah, no problem," I tell her, wondering how to terminate the call without too much embarrassment. But I have to say I *am* feeling uneasy about this.

Hinton continues, "Things are so much more straightforward when you're young, don't you think? I was always comfortable when I thought I was the centre of the universe, but now I'm an adult and it's come as a bit of a shock to me that I'm not. Not the centre of the universe, that is. I mean, I'm right out on the fringes. If I'm a drop in the ocean of the universe, I'm one of the drops that evaporates in the sunlight and reappears as a droplet in a cloud; then the droplet falls as rain, lands on a leaf and gets consumed in one swish of a tapir's tongue. In the telegenic age in which we live, I feel like I'm a pixelated blur. Oh well, forsan miseros meliora sequentur - for those in misery, perhaps better things will follow. Am I making sense, Neil?"

"Not really. What's a tapir?"

"It's not about tapirs. It's about me, my whole personality and everything about me."

I think she's waiting for me to say something reassuring. And, honestly, I try as hard as I can. "Listen, um, don't fret about things, Hinton. Chin up! And I promise if I see a tapir, I'll shoot it. Or, at the very least, I'll give it a stern talking-to."

I knock at the bedroom door again. Still no response from Catfish. This time, I call her name, open the door and walk through to where she quite conspicuously isn't. She's gone. Not a trace of her, apart from a half-eaten carrot omelette and what appears to be the vial of hartglue lying on the bedside cabinet.

Pondering this apparent disaster, my brain does that thing where it twists everything negatively, tighter and tighter, like a rubber band, and then you let go and you're flying around the room in crazy erratic loops and breathtaking climbs and dives, before finally crash-landing on the bed. Okay, I tell myself, settle down, control your breathing and work things out, calmly and methodically. You know what? I tell myself the most ridiculous things sometimes. I think if someone shot me, I'd tell myself not to bleed. Well, *of course* I'm going to panic! Panic! Panic! Panic! What the hell's going on? I'm stuck here all on my own, knowing my entire species is on the brink of destruction, witnessing the damage being inflicted on one of the first victims and all I've got is a small vial of alien chemical stuff. Oh, and the manky remains of a carrot omelette. Come on, you're better than this, I tell myself. This panicky half-wit isn't the real you.

But, actually, it is.

Anyway, yukawa3's disappearance doesn't make a lot of sense, except... well, I suppose he might think he's completed his mission. After all, he's warned me of the danger, prescribed the antidote and delivered the vital chemical thing. I have to accept that I've got everything I need to save the human race and I just need to make it happen. One step at a time. Staring at the carrot omelette, I start to ponder if it's in some way significant. Could he have left it for a reason?

Carrots were the source of one of the great disinformation coups of the Second World War. A particular RAF squadron operated exclusively at night and the British government disseminated and encouraged rumours that the pilots could see in the dark because they ate a lot of carrots. In fact, the squadron was testing a newly developed airborne radar system. The elaborate carrot rumour was cooked up (ha ha) by the British to throw the Germans off the scent.

So, is yukawa3 suggesting something similar? Is my brain capable of developing a disinformation strategy? Is it possible the chilloks could be distracted from what they're doing and become suspicious if we all start planting carrots everywhere? Would they be worried about their primitive distant cousins scurrying about below the ground? No, no, seriously, I must take just one step at a time. Before I think of anything else, I have to speak to Disney and arrange to see her.

The CC chat is short and succinct. Disney is perfectly amenable to meeting up, even at such short notice. So, before the hour is out, here I am, on the monorail hurtling towards Reading. Before the CONNECT observatory was built, the most memorable thing I'd ever heard about Nuneaton is that it's a stop on the monorail between Sheffield and Oxford. Reading is said to be only marginally less boring. Never mind, this isn't supposed to be a holiday.

The rural landscape amazes me. Okay, what amazes me is that there still *is* a rural landscape. Unable to help myself, I call Aysha on my CC. The inevitable bounce-back. It's official – we've had a friendshipectomy. I gaze forlornly at blocks of regimented pines thinning out to make way for rolling hills, then acres and acres of majestic broadleaf woods clinging to slopes that sweep down to a shimmering river. All the autumn colours are there, from rusty browns to bright scarlets: a silent, stunning and tragic drama, featuring a massive cast of dying leaves. The thought occurs to me that whatever it is that compels me towards Aysha is a force that's also driving me insane. Having such feelings for someone entails a fearful and appalling risk. It carries the threat of utter desolation if it's unrequited or if it just goes wrong somehow. And yet this makes the attraction all the more compelling in a perverse sort of way. When two people are mutually crazy about each other, all the pieces fit so easily and so perfectly. When your heart gets broken, however, it can take ages to get the pieces back together.

Clearly, this is a good time to tell myself something. I really need to give myself a good talking-to. Trying to focus on the matter in hand, I take out the vial of hartglue and rehearse my pitch to Disney in my head. Eventually, my thoughts wander. I wonder about the chilloks. How could a species of insect become so fabulously advanced? But thinking about it, humans have been around for maybe a few hundred thousand years at most; insects have been on Earth for at least four hundred *million* years!

I watch a small fly walk upside down on the underside of the luggage rack and contemplate swatting it. Long before a fly leaps, its tiny brain must calculate the location of the impending threat, devise an escape plan and arrange its legs in an optimal position to propel itself out of harm's way in the opposite direction. And all of this must occur within a few milliseconds of spotting the danger. Is that impressive, or what? Sensory information being processed *unbelievably* efficiently to trigger an immediate motor response.

And now chilloks have evolved to the point where they have overtaken (and can potentially destroy) all other life forms in the known universe. But can I really do anything about it? I mean, look at me. Checking my reflection in the train window, I'm shocked at what I see. I know it's just a reflection in a train window and it's obviously blurry and indistinct, but, hell, I'm scruffy, unshaven and it looks like the life has drained out of me. Come on, do I look like the sort of person who might save everyone on the planet? Neil of Nuneaton, superhero. Don't think so somehow.

I put the vial away and pick up my hat. One quick flick of the wrist and the fly is swatted into messy oblivion. "Hah!" I exclaim loudly, causing all heads to turn towards me. I shrug. "This is a no-fly zone," I tell the man sitting opposite me.

Disney meets me at the station. Flouncing along the platform in her retro-hippie ensemble - cropped black leather jacket over a pale chambray dress, one hand over her fringed boho-chic bag, the other holding her pink floppy hat - she greets me with a beaming smile and a hug, but forgets my name. "Hi Noel," she says breezily. "That's good timing. I've just got here from my yoga class." As the weather is fine, she suggests a short stroll along the Thames on the way to her laboratory.

The urgent, clamorous honking of Canada Geese shatters the peace as we walk along the path towards the meadow. A large flock is grazing and preening on the bank. Overhead, another flock is flying in V-formation, heading south over the railway.

"Interesting thing about geese," says Disney, stopping to admire them. "As each bird flaps its wings, it creates uplift for the birds following behind. Also, if you watch them over a period of time, you'll see that they swap positions a lot and the flock has no constant leader."

I hope this is a good omen. I could really do with someone to share the burden I'm carrying right now. I nod in agreement.

"Yeah, I don't know about you," she goes on, "but I believe there are lots of lessons we can learn from nature. Like those geese, people who share a common sense of purpose can get where they're going quicker and easier if they harness the strength of the whole group."

"Hmm," I say, "I suppose that's true in lots of situations."

"*All* situations," Disney insists with a fervour I find perplexing. "Cooperation is everything. You'll never get anywhere worth going unless you pull together."

"Okay." Wary of getting into any kind of quarrel with her, I grin with phony acquiescence, but my mind says, "Those who act like sheep get eaten by wolves." I say it aloud. Damn it! Why do I have to say it aloud?

"No, no, no!" she insists with a beguiling smile that masks an underlying hint of something steely and uncompromising. "This cuts to the very core of everything about us."

The ensuing debate takes us all the way out of the meadow, up Westfield Road and through the gates of the Balmore Institute of Pharmaceutical Science. It ranges from flocks of geese and lone wolves all the way to the lotus leaf and the hermaphroditic clownfish. Never have lessons from nature been so full of contradictory assertions and metaphorical ardour.

"Anyway," says Disney, her passion for the subject unquenched and apparently insatiable. "It's actually unusual for a wolf to live and hunt alone, because wolves are naturally social animals." She laughs and the dimple on her cheek becomes even more pronounced.

By the time we've knocked back a couple of watermelon and strawberry lemonades in Disney's office, we've given air to all kinds of fundamental socio-political questions, like how much unbridled 'free market' is needed for economic growth and what degree of government interference is acceptable to prevent morally unacceptable outcomes. All of it illustrated with examples from the natural world. It's engrossing, yes, but I'm beginning to despair of ever getting round to discussing the antidote. Is it my fault? Am I just scared to broach the subject? Suddenly Disney glances at her CC and stands up. "Sorry, it's my sister," she says. "It's Hinton. I have to take this."

She leaves the room and I have time to reconsider my approach. Clearly, if I continue to allow Disney to go off at tangents all the time, she'll be like a moth in a factory full of light bulbs. I resolve to stick to direct questions and avoid references to any peripheral subjects. And I decide to avoid the extraterrestrial factor. Keep it simple.

When she returns, her expression is cloudier. "I'll be coming back with you on the train," she says. "I've got to look in on Hinton."

"Oh, right. Is everything okay?" I ask.

"You don't know?"

"Know what?"

"She overdosed on sleeping pills."

"No way!" I'm so shocked I can't speak for a few seconds. "When? Is she okay?"

"We were all at the Blood Moon Party," Disney explains. "She stayed at home and took a whole bunch of pills and wasn't found till the next day. Er, yesterday. But she's okay. They gave her plenty of fluids and she came round. Aysha's staying with her at the moment." She shrugs. "Well, this is where we have to do like the geese."

Perplexed and worried, I just shake my head in confusion.

She goes on. "When one goose gets sick or gets shot down or something, two geese drop out of formation and follow it down to the ground to provide help and protection. And they stay with the stricken bird until it can fly again. At times like this we have to do the same."

She's right. Damn geese. Damn stupid animal analogies. Thank God Hinton didn't succeed in the suicide attempt. If that's what it was. But this gives an incredible fresh urgency to my mission. I suddenly realise something. "I spoke to her this morning!"

"Oh yes, of course! That's how you got my comm-ID. Did she sound okay?"

I nod. "Well, she seemed a bit down, I guess." I paraphrase the conversation Hinton and I had, carefully avoiding any allusion to me shooting a tapir.

NO BIG DEAL

The most striking feature of Balmore Park is the view south over the city of Reading. Formerly known as Balmers Field, this hill was the scene of a bloody battle fought during the Civil War. Skirmishes between Royalists and Parliamentary forces defending Caversham Bridge were so fierce, it's said that 'the dew fell red with blood'.

Disney's knowledge of the local history is impressive and fascinating. Inspirational, actually. Almost daunting. I get a bit caught up in it. History is so cool. I love history. Each day that comes along is the anniversary of a whole array of totally fascinating events.

"I could have been a historian," I boast. Did I really say that? It's a claim I cannot possibly justify. I might just as well have declared an interest in being an amateur brain surgeon.

"Really? So why *didn't* you? Mmm?" she drawls.

Okay, the game's up. "Well, I... I didn't, y'know, take history at school or college or, y'know, whatever."

"You shouldn't let that stop you," says Disney, splendidly delivering me from my embarrassment. "The purpose of school and college is not to educate you, but to fire you up to educate *yourself* throughout the rest of your life."

"That is so true," I concur. "There are three rules for getting the most out of your life and that's one of them."

Disney has a curious look in her eyes. "What are the other two?"

I've no idea why I didn't anticipate that question. "Yeah, I... Well, that's certainly one of them."

I guess I'm nervous. I have no other explanation for my abysmal failure to come across as a sentient being. Anyway, the time for curves and tangents has passed. It's got to be straight lines from now on. Producing the vial of hartglue from my pocket, I thrust it in Disney's hand with the words, "I think this is unbelievably important. But I don't know what it is."

"And you want to find out what it is and *why* it's important."

"Yes."

"Do you know *anything* about it? Anything at all? Like, what makes you *think* it's important?" Sensing my growing impatience, she changes her mind about asking more questions and heads for the door. "I'll get our guys to look at it right away," she promises. "Help yourself to tea."

While she's gone, I fret about stuff. I fret about Aysha, who I now realise must have been present during my CC chat with Hinton this morning. Then I remind myself I've got far more important things to fret about and, anyway, I guess you shouldn't make room in your life for people who don't want to be there. So I fret about Hinton. I fret about my decision to keep yukawa3's visit to myself (although the media would have been like a pit bull with a rag doll and, anyway, I *did* try to tell Aysha). And, yes, I kind of vaguely fret about the survival of everyone on the planet. Well, you have to really, don't you?

The vertical rays of the midday sun bathe the sprawling cityscape in a harsh light. Red and white and grey, the cranes and towers and skyscrapers seem to be abandoned from this distance, the teeming bustle and snarled traffic nothing more than an obscure assumption.

What really bothers me is this: assuming a viable antidote can be produced in mass quantities, what about the logistics of getting it distributed and administered globally in a short period of time? Hmm. Now *that's* something to fret about.

The door opens, shaking me out of my thoughts. Disney crosses the room, sits at her desk and taps her fingers in a slow and quiet rhythm. "It's a solution containing a neurotransmitter that we're not familiar with," she says. "We've isolated it and we're carrying out some more tests."

I nod. "I was told it's called hartglue."

"It seems to be some kind of MAOI."

"Oh, okay," I nod again, trying to appear as wise and learned as possible. "That's interesting."

Disney rumbles me right away, but continues with elegant politeness. "Monoamine oxidase inhibitor," she clarifies. "Monoamine oxidase is a metabolic enzyme that mops up neurotransmitters from the synapse once they've transferred a signal to the postsynaptic neuron. These, er, hartglue molecules appear to inhibit the activity of MAO. Basically, in layman's terms, they might have the effect of prolonging people's emotional responses for long periods."

"What's a synapse?"

"Well, very simply put, a synapse is the junction between two neurons."

I ponder this with all the intellectual energy of an Aristotle. Or one of his statues anyway. "Right, so, simply put, what's a neuron?"

"It's a specialised nerve cell that receives, processes, and transmits information to other cells in the body."

Rising to the challenge of translating this into a concept I can actually wrap my brain around, I think I come up with something vaguely plausible: "So basically, they're bits of your body that tell other bits of your body what to do." Yes, I think I've pretty much nailed it there, so I check Disney's eyes for a sign of approval. "I'm grasping this pretty well, don't you think?"

"Truthfully?" asks Disney, a mischievous twinkle in her eye betraying her enjoyment. "Yeah, no, I'm sorry, I think you're one neuron short of a synapse. Sorry."

As insults go, it probably ranks quite high in the scientific hall of shame, but, I'm kind of okay with it. Anyway, I've tried my hardest to gain her trust. It's time to get down to brass tacks. "Can I run something by you?"

Disney leans back in her chair, steeples her fingers and presses them to her lips. "Sure," she says.

"Hypothetical situation," I begin. "Let's just say, for argument's sake, that this hartglue is a key component of a cure for a global epidemic."

"Pandemic," says Disney, correcting me. "If it's global, it's a pandemic. And, uh, should I be worried?"

"Just hypothetical," I assure her. "What steps would the pharmaceutical industry have to take to get it approved? Let's assume it's really urgent - the disease is serious and it's spreading quickly."

Disney breathes out through her nose, a soft snort of amusement. "But what disease? What pandemic? If there was a pandemic, I'm pretty sure I'd know something about it by now. Yeah, okay, I know – hypothetical. Well, what hypothetical treatments are already out there for this hypothetical disease?"

It won't hurt to tell Disney everything yukawa3 said about the antidote. "Well, anything that releases dopamine, serotonin, oxytocin and endorphins in sufficient quantities will work. But, as I understand it, the hartglue molecule is the thing that will keep these happy chemicals in people's systems. Without it, they disappear?"

"Okay," says Disney. "That makes sense. That's exactly what an effective MAOI will do."

"So are you saying that the first thing you have to do is compare it against the best currently available treatment? Is that it?"

"Actually, no," says Disney, shrugging with something approaching embarrassment. "You're going to lurve this. You don't actually have to prove that it's better than other treatments."

I'm more than a little surprised. "You don't? Really? Why not?"

She lights a cigarette and goes on to explain that, even when effective treatments are already available, the drug regulators are happy for a company simply to show that its drug is better than nothing.

"Better than nothing?" I'm flabbergasted (and I hate using that word). "So, what does that even really mean?"

"It means a company only has to demonstrate that the drug works better than a dummy placebo."

"A placebo?"

"Yeah. Better than a pill with *no* medicine in it. It might seem very strange, but you just have to show that your new drug is better than a placebo."

"Wow."

"Obviously, you'd have to prove your drug doesn't introduce new side effects."

"Obviously."

Stubbing out her cigarette, Disney fixes me with her deep brown eyes inherited from her half-Japanese father. "Let's go to the lab and see what else they've found."

First, we call in on the lab assistant in the small office just across the hall. He's in his late fifties, tall and stocky with bushy eyebrows, muttonchop whiskers and grey hair balding on top. After brief introductions, he shakes his head slowly and speaks in a low, stern voice: "Wasted time is wasted money."

"Now then, Robert, we always waste time wisely here," Disney admonishes him with a good-humoured smile. "Every experience is an opportunity to learn and grow."

When Robert folds his arms, the sleeves of his lab coat ride up revealing tattoos on his forearms. I believe one of them is a picture of the Greek philosopher, Diogenes of Sinope. He glowers at Disney and she glowers right back. "Why are we bothering to analyse this stuff?" he demands. "If you ask me it's much the same thing as the anandamide you find in chocolate. Yes, I said chocolate. Waste of time."

"That can't be right!" I protest. "It's really special stuff. *Really* special. I *know* it is."

"Like I said," the assistant growls, "you can find it in chocolate. Some of the guys replicated the solution and tested it orally. It's no big deal."

Disney lets out a gasp of disconcerted surprise. "They drank it?"

"It's safe," says Robert. "Like chocolate. Really. It's no big deal."

The three of us walk over to the lab. As we approach the glass partition, a bizarre sight meets our eyes. The entire team of lab technicians are cavorting around the benches, stools and cabinets as if they're dancing to a polka being played by a heavy metal band. Pointed elbows, arms thrashing around, thumbs tucked under armpits, chins poking in and out, they look like a flock of scalded chickens. Wait, I think this looks familiar. I've seen this before. Surely not! Oh yes, this is yukawa3's herky-jerky turkey dance.

"Okay now it's a big deal," Robert concedes with a weary sigh.

Disney's expression tells me she won't tolerate any more hypothetical questions. "Where did you get this stuff?" she says. "I think you need to tell me more about it."

"I will," I promise. "But, first, can I just ask you what you'd do if there really was a pandemic and you'd have to manufacture vast quantities of an antidote very quickly."

"We're cutting edge here," she asserts, running her fingers through her hair in a gesture of vexation. "We use high-yield cell-based production technology and we can make vast quantities in a relatively short period of time."

"What about testing?"

"It depends."

"On what?"

"What the time constraints are. Sometimes there just isn't enough time to complete all the clinical testing you'd normally do. It just depends. Why? Come on, tell me, what's going on?"

I refrain from telling her I'm trying to save the world. I just tell her, "I want to save your sister."

THE FOOTBRIDGE

We wave our arms to get our microchip implants scanned and run full pelt along the platform, dodging passengers and suitcases on remote controlled trolleys. Moments later we're gliding off on the monorail train back to Nuneaton. Disney immerses herself in CC conversations, leaving me to reflect on an interesting day. Prior to this trip, the prospect of getting an antidote ready and distributed in a narrow window of time had filled me with billowing waves of unease and trepidation. I just can't believe how straightforward it might now prove to be. The pharmaceutical industry seems to be regulated with all the rigour of an amateur pantomime. Astonished as I was to hear about the success criteria applied to drug trials, I was simply flabbergasted (oh no! That word again!) to learn from Robert that trials that produce negative results are not even published because… well, because they don't have to be! When a project to search for extraterrestrial life is subject to more red tape than you can shake a stick at, it seems extraordinary to me that the pharmaceutical industry, of all things, can be so lax and haphazardly regulated.

Another thing. There's a paradox here. Disney refuses to give the antidote to her sister even though her own technicians have approved it as safe. (Well, to be clear, they've approved it now that they've made adjustments to the dosage – their initial results were quite spectacular!)

When it came to it, I couldn't possibly tell Disney about chilloks and braintuning and so on, so I suggested to her that Hinton's problems are due to chronic serotonin depletion. Although she totally accepts this diagnosis and acknowledges the viability of the antidote, she's adamant that we must seek a different cure. I just don't understand that. The foibles and idiosyncrasies of the industry appear to filter down to the people employed in it. Anyway, the events of the day have left me with the inverse of the problem I faced at the start of it. The speedy development and implementation of an effective antidote on a global scale might be straightforward, but ensuring the survival of one particular individual (Hinton) might not be. So, *now* what do I do?

The train seems to be travelling much faster this evening. The vista I enjoyed earlier in the day is now out of focus, blurred and distorted. Bits of mist are shrouding the hills. The sheep flash past so fast, there's no opportunity to count them. I fall asleep anyway.

When Disney gently shakes me awake, we've arrived in Nuneaton and it's getting dark. We make our way back to the observatory complex on foot.

"It's weird that you won't let Hinton take the antidote," I say as we walk across the car park towards the main road, where a couple of hovercars speed away into the distance.

"I won't take any risks with my sister."

I'm tempted to challenge her to explain why she's prepared to take risks with the rest of the world's population… but I don't. The irony, however, is as obvious as a neon-lit billboard in the middle of a desert.

To be fair, she does her best to clarify how she feels about it. "Look at this road, for example," she says. "If there's a million-to-one chance of being hit by a car while crossing it, you'd deem it relatively safe, wouldn't you? That's fair enough. So would I. But, metaphorically speaking, I've got a vulnerable child in my arms."

"You mean your sister?"

"Yes. And I tell you what – I'm going to take the footbridge."

I'm confused. "There isn't a footbridge."

"It's a metaphorical footbridge."

"Okay. I get what you're saying. It's just not a very good analogy."

"Why not?"

"She might jump off it."

I probably shouldn't have said that. I get a punch in the ribs and it's not a metaphorical one.

Disney has arranged to meet Hinton and Aysha in the Mars Bar. We arrive before them and order a couple of drinks. It's pointless really, but I ask her one more time about her reluctance to give Hinton the antidote. "A few days back you told me you have to play the cards that life deals you," I say. "Well, it seems to me this thing with Hinton is a rubbish hand. And now life's just dealt you a wild card. Why not take a chance on it? You don't strike me as someone who's content to let fear decide your fate. Sometimes you've just got to take a leap of faith, haven't you?"

"Yeah, but we're not talking about my fate. We're talking about *her* fate. It's one thing to take a leap of faith and hope your parachute opens. It's quite another to push *someone else* out of a plane."

"I just hope you don't end up being haunted by regret."

"Hmm," she says grimly. "But that works both ways."

I contemplate making a small hop of faith myself and telling her all about yukawa3 and the chilloks and the whole nine yards. But I can't do it. I just don't think she's in the right place to hear this right now. Or maybe it's me. Maybe *I* don't feel right about it. Not just yet. So, for a moment, I just listen absently to the clinking of glasses and the hum of conversation punctuated with sporadic bursts of raucous banter. Then I look at her twisting her hands nervously and I decide to tell her a little piece of the truth. I tell her that we've successfully detected extraterrestrial intelligence.

She smiles pleasantly and sips from her glass. "That's great for the project," she responds.

"Wonderful. You say it's a secret? So, why are you telling *me* about it now?"

"Well, because when I was a small boy…" And I tell her the story about me as a four-year-old releasing my balloon dog into the sky in the hope that I might make a friend from a distant planet.

"And now you think your faith has been vindicated."

"Well, yes," I reply.

Disney takes another sip, stares into space for a moment and continues: "But then, it wasn't really *you* taking the leap of faith, was it? It was your balloon dog. And what actually happened to him, do you suppose?"

"Um, he'll have kept floating higher and higher until the difference in the pressure inside and outside… was such that… he would've… y'know..."

She completes the sentence for me. "Exploded!"

"Yeah," I'm forced to concede.

"Not a very good analogy," she says, turning her face to me, revealing a troubled brow and melancholy eyes.

When I see Aysha coming through the door with Hinton, a strange, unsettling feeling starts pounding away in the pit of my stomach. The hurt that I thought might have dissipated by now wells up and, for a moment or two, I find it difficult to even look at her. Wow. I wasn't expecting to feel like this. I guess I'm tipping over into the negative side of accepting the relationship, such as it is, is over. I've always thought that it's important to address such feelings, lest they become toxic to one's wellbeing. At best, emotional suppression is a short-term band-aid; at worst, it just adds to the pain. Anyway, I can't deal with this now. I just can't.

I say 'hi' to Aysha and give Hinton a big hug. Disney does the same.

Totally unprompted, Hinton says she's upset because someone criticised her for parking her hovercar outside the marked lines of a parking bay. Before I can stop myself, I start gushing a whole bunch of stuff you don't say to someone who's depressed. I tell her that life isn't fair. I tell her she's strong and she'll be fine. If only I could have stopped there. But no, I have to go on and on about what a beautiful day it's been and why we all have so many things to be thankful for. I tell her to forget about her troubles for now and have some fun. And I insist on buying her a cocktail.

Hinton, whose edgy angled bob looks a little less-than-sleek-and-shiny this evening, frowns. "There's nothing wrong with my parking. And I'll just have some water, please."

As I start to get up, Disney puts her hand on my shoulder. "I'll get these," she insists.

"So," says Aysha, "you've been swannin' off to Readin'. You were spos'd to be in a meetin' this afternoon."

"What meeting?" I ask.

"The preliminary feasibility review of disclosure formalities. You accepted the invite."

"What was the outcome?"

"Actually," says Aysha, embarrassed, "I'm not sure. Do you know what was decided, Hinton?"

"Yes, of course," Hinton replies, as she settles on a cushioned floaty next to me. "We decided that the Communication Strategy people will make presentations to External Relations and vice versa. So for now we're maintaining the status quo."

"I didn't miss much then," I smile smugly. "We'll be doing that till way past the time the quo has lost its status."

Aysha raises her eyebrows. "You sound a bit jaded."

"Yeah, sorry, I just… I just think progress on this project has become inversely proportional to the number of meetings we have. Nothing gets done. And it gets not done in triplicate! We should change the corporate slogan. How about 'Never put off until tomorrow what you can avoid altogether'?"

"You have to work the system," says Hinton.

"I *do* work the system," I protest.

Aysha shakes her head as if to say 'just leave it'. The smile that accompanies that conspiratorial shake of the head confuses me. Is it a kind of tentative attempt to reestablish the connection between us?

Anyway, Hinton's right. I hate meetings, but I suppose they're a necessary evil. I should probably try to contribute more effectively in them instead of getting all fired up like I'm inclined to do. I don't have a great track record. There was the time I stood up in a meeting and urged everyone to be passionate and always give 110 percent. Hmm. They were statisticians.

Disney returns with the drinks and we chat away pleasantly for a while. I notice Hinton seems to cut a more cheerful figure as the evening wears on. Before long, she's humming along with the background music, lowering the floaty so she can tap her feet, even permitting herself the odd smile.

When Disney reappears from a cigarette break, Hinton stands up with a glazed, beatific smile on her face, her hips swaying along to the rhythm of the music. Aysha turns to her and says, "I love those purple trousers. Where did you get them?"

"They're not really purple," Hinton says, slapping Aysha gently on the thigh. "They're more like a mixture of red and blue!" With that, she throws her head back and hoots with laughter like a gibbon with a whole crate of bananas.

Disney and I exchange glances. Leaning over to me in an attempt to be discreet, she whispers, "I took a leap of faith."

BIG LEAP OF FAITH

My apartment door closes behind me as doors are wont to do. I scan the room for anything that's changed since the last time I was here. No, everything looks the same. Except the fish. I'm sure the fish are swimming in different directions. The whole scene has an eerie, surreal quality. That was definitely one cocktail too many.

Seriously, something feels strange around here. Perhaps it's me. Perhaps I'm having to reevaluate things after this evening. It's possible, for example, that Hinton isn't on a slippery slope of chillok-induced brain erosion after all. It's possible she just slipped into a bad episode and now she's back again. And I've just realised – yep, I'm pretty sure no one spoke a word of Latin the whole time. Everything definitely seemed more normal tonight. But if that's true, isn't it also possible that all yukawa3's gloomy forebodings are without foundation and we're *not* facing the great catastrophe he warned me about and... and if *that*'s true, isn't it also possible that he... that he, you know, didn't really warn me about *anything at all*? In other words, could I have just imagined the whole yukawa3 thing? Isn't it possible that my mind was disturbed, racked with guilt about inviting a strange woman back to my apartment? I could have had a psychological meltdown and yukawa3 was just a manifestation of my abnormal and befuddled mental state.

That would be, uh, annoying. Sorry, I'll think of a better word later. Oh God! I'm starting to see this as Aysha will have seen it. Yes, you remember Aysha! Aysha Malik, the renowned astrophysicist. I'm sure I've mentioned her. Remember, I told you a while back that I hoped we'd become better friends and then we didn't, because I messed up, and now it looks like we might again. Oh come on, keep up! The curious thing about this was her behaviour this evening. You see, she seemed relaxed and fairly friendly towards me and... and why exactly is the handle of the bedroom door turning?

A warbly, mechanical sound emanates through the door like the voice of a horribly corroded robot being sick. I look around frantically, and at first I see nothing that I can use as a weapon, then after a moment or two I still can't see anything. Slowly but perceptibly, the sound transforms into a recognisable voice speaking recognisable words: "Brace yourself, my friend. The awesome and imposing figure you're about to behold may prove too much."

As the door opens, I can see precisely nothing at all because I've rolled behind the sofa.

"No, come out. Come out, Neil," the voice, which has become a strangely strangulated and reedy one, implores me. "It's just me, yukawa3. But please be aware, I'm not in an earthling disguise any longer."

Drawing myself up on my knees, I peer over the top of the sofa and blink several times to assure myself my eyes are in fact open and I'm not having a nightmare. Yukawa3 just looks like a fairly regular guy. Standing in front of the bedroom door is a tall, bipedal, vaguely humanoid creature with large, coal-black, almond-shaped eyes. The smooth, bluish-grey, oily skin isn't scaly, but might nevertheless be described as lizard-like. There are no external ears or genitalia and the mouth is small and pinched. Thin, wiry arms reach almost to the knee. Okay, so I was lying - he doesn't look like a regular guy at all. I've seen Gene Taylor after a really bad weekend bender and if you took away the beard... no, seriously, nothing could have prepared me for this.

"I'm *not* staring," I say before my brain resumes its normal functions.

"I didn't accuse you of staring."

"Okay, I can see why you were so keen to retrieve your yellow sou'wester." I say, recovering my equilibrium. "No doubt about it - it really must do something for your appearance."

"Thanks. It's the prominent cheekbones."

"Well, you'd better tell me what the hell happened," I suggest. "You kind of left me in the lurch. Why did you leave? And, also, thinking about it, why did you come back? And a bonus question – why are you looking like that?"

Yukawa3 settles himself on the sofa, folding one thin, rubbery leg over the other like a puppet made of, er, rubber. "I decided to revert to my native form to help you persuade your friend Aysha that everything we told her is true."

"You didn't need to *leave* though, did you? And why didn't you tell me you were going? I thought you'd gone for good."

"I didn't think you'd want to witness the mutation. It's not like a butterfly emerging from a chrysalis, you know. It's more like a Frankenstein monster turning into a huge malignant tumour and swallowing an active particle accelerator pellet. I'm exaggerating, of course, but it kind of *feels* like that. Anyway, I thought I left you a perfectly clear message that I'd be back shortly."

"You did?"

"I left a half-eaten carrot omelette in the bedroom. I was letting you know I'd be back to finish my supper."

"Ah. So, you weren't suggesting I mount a disinformation campaign designed to confuse and distract the chilloks?" It now dawns on me that all my zealous efforts to go viral with the carrot message on social media have been totally in vain.

"You got that from an unfinished carrot omelette?" asks yukawa3, making a popping, vibrating sound with his lips. Actually, he doesn't really *have* lips, so, whatever. Still recuperating from the after-effects of HDA, he seems tired and brings his knobbly fingers to his lips as he yawns, revealing a total absence of teeth. "There's another reason I had to go back to Smolin9," he says. "I had to break the news about your grandmother's cremation to polkingbeal67."

"How did he take it?" I enquire.

"Well, let's just say he's now licking his wounds."

"Metaphorically, I assume."

"No, no, physically. He slammed a door."

"How did that hurt him physically?"

"His hand was in it," yukawa3 explains, wincing at the recollection. "Then he became so angry about breaking his hand, he kicked a plant."

As yukawa3 winces again, I have to ask: "Don't tell me that hurt him physically too?"

"He was barefoot and it was a cactus. He's declared war on your planet."

"What? Just because my grandmother was cremated? That's ridiculous. You can't declare war on an entire planet for something like that."

"I agree." Yukawa3 shook his head ruefully and slumped back in the sofa. "To be honest, I think it's *my* fault, because he thought I was laughing about it. I wasn't, but, to be fair, I can see why he thought that."

"Why? What did you say?"

"I explained about his heart being cremated and he kind of instinctively clutched at his chest. So, I… I asked him if he had heartburn."

I bite my lip, but nothing can suppress the snorts of laughter that erupt from me.

"You do realise the declaration of war is a very serious matter?" he says, exhaling loudly and motioning to my CC. "Anyway, aren't you going to call your friend and get her over here? I hope I haven't gone through all this for nothing."

"I would, but Aysha's CC is configured to reject my calls."

"Oh, I forgot!" Yukawa3's hand flies to his mouth and he sucks in a breath.

"Forgot what? You couldn't have known about her CC."

"Your earthling devices are very primitive, but it's possible to reconfigure them remotely with a microwocky."

An uneasy feeling creeps into my brain. "Are you saying what I think you're saying? *You* reconfigured Aysha's CC to bounce my calls?"

"I meant to switch it back, but I forgot all about it." A singular look of sheepishness spreads over yukawa3's face.

"But why?" I ask with a significant degree of indignation, unable to put this into any kind of context.

"Sorry," he says. "Honey trap. Implementation script, second stage, subsection entitled 'Impede Potential Rivals'. I identified Aysha as a threat as soon as I arrived."

"Do the remote thing. Change it back, please," I instruct, striving to maintain a veneer of polite restraint.

Yukawa3 shakes his head. "It's out of range."

I call Disney instead and ask her to come over with Aysha. Even though I give no reason for the invitation, she probably detects something in my voice and readily agrees to come along straight away. Several minutes elapse during which total silence prevails between me and yukawa3. After what seems like an eternity, there's a knock on the door.

Obviously I have to prepare them for what they're about to encounter. "Hi. Before you come in, I must warn you that there's something here, someone here who… Just brace yourselves for a bit of a shock."

I open the door to let them in. Despite the warning, Disney glances at yukawa3, lets out a bloodcurdling scream and both she and Aysha involuntarily jump back towards the hallway.

"It's okay," I assure them. "You're perfectly safe. Take your time. Come on in when you're ready."

"Good evening," says yukawa3, flashing an aggrieved look at them. "I'm not offended, not at all. I would like to have made a better first impression, but hey. Actually we've already met. I'm the person you knew as Catfish." Drawing himself up to his full height, he takes a step towards them and pouts. At least, I think it's a pout. Extending a hand towards them, he adds, "I'm yukawa3, special envoy from Smolin9. It is spoken."

When they recover enough composure to close their mouths, Disney and Aysha hug each other, then they grasp the grotesquely long, pliable limb in front of them, screech a couple of inarticulate greetings and hug each other again. Finally, we all settle down around the kitchen table. Between us, yukawa3 and I proceed to spill the entire story, much of which, of course, Aysha has heard before.

"I just realised something!" Disney exclaims, her voice almost shrill with excitement. "Lambda! The balloon dog!"

"What about it?" asks yukawa3, completely baffled.

"Oh nothing," says Disney, grinning at me like the cat that ate the canary. "Neil knows what I mean. Something that happened when he was a boy." I assume she's joined up a few dots in her mind and skewed everything into some kind of bizarre conclusion.

"So, there you have it," I conclude, giving Aysha a tight-lipped smile.

"I have a few questions," Disney announces, turning to yukawa3. "You say my sister has been afflicted with this nasty braintuning thing. How do you know the three of us here have not had *our* brains infiltrated?"

"My microwocky can detect the presence of cerebrum ambulans within a radius of five of your earthling kilometres." Flicking and prodding his microwocky, he grunts and whistles and declares, "Nothing. No trace. All clear. I hope that answers your question."

"Wait a minute," I say, as a thought pokes up its head like a startled meerkat. "Did you say five kilometres?"

When yukawa3 nods, it looks for all the world like his head is going to snap off.

I turn to Disney. "Where is Hinton right now?"

With a smile as broad as a slice of melon, she leans over, hugs me and replies, "We left her in the bar. She was *dancing* and *laughing*, Neil. *Dancing* and *laughing*!"

The penny drops. "Oh, I see. You gave her the antidote! So that's what you meant when you told me you took a leap of faith."

"I slipped it into her drink." She turns once again to yukawa3. "Why do you suppose they chose my sister? Why weren't *we* targeted?"

I haven't had much time to acquaint myself with Mortian facial expressions, but as far as I can tell, yukawa3 looks unaccountably buoyant and cheerful. "Our experts believe they go for easy targets first. During the first wave of invasion, they ignore people with elevated levels of happy chemicals in the brain. You're a content and optimistic person who spends a lot of time in, er, timeless zones where you enjoy the photon energy pouring into the world, so I think you were considered a poor candidate..." He waves a bulbous fingertip at me and Aysha. "...and these two have constantly raised levels of oxytocin. They're in love with one another."

Aysha and I glance at each other and do a double take. To be honest, Aysha looks ready to fall over. "How can you possibly know somethin' like that?" she asks.

"Well, for some time now we've been studying cultural and behavioural aspects of earthling humanity. Stuff like language, style of dress, eating habits and so on. But also the effects of emotions such as love, fear, anger and grief on your social interactions. It really didn't take me long to identify many of the classic psychological, behavioural and physiological indicators of emotional arousal."

"Like what?" asks Aysha, eyes wide with disbelief and astonishment.

Yukawa3 starts to squirm a little under Aysha's intense scrutiny. "Well, for example, er, jealousy and, er, signs of irrational thinking. You demonstrated anxious attachment to Neil by your hostility towards me when I first arrived."

I think we're *all* starting to squirm now.

"And I've been *irrational*?" Aysha enquires. Her voice contains so many undertones of animosity that I'm sure we all consider diving for cover.

"Certainly." Yukawa3 is clearly determined to reassert an air of authority. "Verily. You were presented with all the facts relating to the chilloks and my mission here on Earth. Don't you remember the occasion - I was literally pulling my hair out? Neil and I told you everything honestly, sensibly and soberly. And you refused to believe any of it. Irrational. It is spoken."

"You got me down as irrational from me not believin' *that* story?"

Then suddenly, out of the blue, she turns towards me with a smile so radiant it lights up the room and takes my breath away. "And as fer you," she says, tipping her head to one side. "what 'ave you got to say fer yerself? Hmm?"

The hairs on the back of my neck stand up. "Buckle up, Babe!" I tell her, shooting her a knowing look.

No, I don't. Of course I don't. What I actually say is: "Well, I've been meaning to say, y'know… Yeah, he's right. Y'know, the oxytocin thing." It's moments like this when you need someone to prompt you: "Go on, Neil! This is the part where you kiss her!" But Disney doesn't prompt me and yukawa3 doesn't prompt me. And anyway, real life isn't some corny twentieth century Hollywood movie. I smile back at Aysha. Yes, that'll do for now. Sorry. Just a smile.

Silence descends for a moment or two while we all try to digest what's happening (there's plenty of loud thinking going on though – in fact, it's really noisy in my head). Pale lights start flashing on yukawa3's microwocky and, for a moment or two, his eyes, mind and fingers become totally absorbed in the mysterious device.

I'm the first to speak. "Well, I guess we've got to talk about manufacturing and distributing the antidote. There's a world out there that needs saving."

"No longer necessary," mumbles yukawa3, not looking up from the microwocky.

None of us say anything. So much to say, no way of saying it. I mean, how can he drop something like that and then just sit there ignoring us? Anyway, eventually I give in. Sighing in exasperation, I ask him, "Okay, why's it no longer necessary? What are you talking about?"

"They've gone," says yukawa3, still not looking up. "The chilloks have abandoned the invasion."

"Why?" asks Disney.

"How do you know?" asks Aysha.

"Why don't you take your face out of that damn microwocky thing and tell us what the hell is going on?" I ask. I don't really, but I feel like it.

"It was the same on our planet," he says, turning his face towards us at last. "You only need to win one battle and you win the war. With us, it was polkingbeal67. And here on Earth, it's Hinton. You gave her the antidote and it worked and the chilloks have just given up on the whole thing."

Disney and Aysha squeal and hug. Then they squeal and hug again. As for me, I glance at my reflection in the mirror on the wall by the bedroom door. So the sort of person who's capable of saving everyone on the planet really *does* look like this. Okay, technically, Disney administered the antidote, but hey. Take a bow, Neil of Nuneaton, superhero!

There's nothing alcoholic in my apartment, so, to mark the occasion and celebrate our success, I crack open a bottle of carrot juice.

Yukawa3 sits up very straight and coughs. "I have almost completed my mission here and I must leave." he intones rather pompously.

"Almost?" I ask him. "What do you mean by almost?"

"Our planets are at war. And I was… I was wondering if you would consider coming back to Smolin9 with me to act as a peace ambassador representing your planet. Through your grandmother, you have a connection with our planet and a personal connection with our revered leader, polkingbeal67. I believe you can make him see sense."

"Do you mean now? As in *right* now?" I ask, sensing an urgency in his voice.

"Right now," he confirms. "In about five of your earthling minutes. The coordinates have been processed. It's all about to happen and it's too late to cancel."

What follows is the proverbial pin-dropping quiet thing. No one says a word until finally Aysha gently clutches my arm and whispers, "You're not going without me!" The hairs on the back of my neck stand up once again.

Yukawa3 nods. "You can all come," he confirms.

"Don't look at me," says Disney, throwing up her hands. "I'm not going anywhere."

"Our planet has two suns," says yukawa3. "There's twice as much photon energy for you to enjoy."

Unconvinced, Disney shakes her head. "*I'm* not going anywhere," she repeats emphatically.

I have to say something. I just don't know what, so I appeal to Disney and Aysha, "Is no one going to talk me out of this?" I know - a bit lame, but it's all I've got right now.

Yukawa3 turns to me and Aysha. "So you two are *both* coming?" he asks. We glance at each other and nod and he hands us a vial of colourless liquid. "Drink it," he says. "It's HDA and you have to take it."

All that remains is for us to say our goodbyes to Disney, whose eyes start to fill with tears. She hugs Aysha, turns to me and says, "It all sounds so insane and dangerous. You must be very uncertain about this. I just wish there was a footbridge." Her voice gets smaller and smaller. "But I guess you've got to do it. Go ahead. Take your leap of faith."

She's right, I tell myself. I must take this leap of faith and follow in the wake of that pink balloon dog I released in my childhood, even if it means… well, engaging with the land of the herky-jerky turkey dance, for one thing!

"We'll be sure to fly in V-formation," I reassure her, handing her a spare key to the apartment. "Please ask Hinton to look after my fish."

Aysha, yukawa3 and I link hands. The idea of travelling to another world may turn out to be the most gargantuan lapse of judgement of my entire life, but right now I feel like I can take on any challenge in any world with one hand, as long as Aysha is holding the other one. Suddenly, she and yukawa3 vanish like burst bubbles.

Uh oh. I'm still here. Has something gone wrong? "Hey!" I call out, pointlessly. "What's going on?" Then I start disintegrating into a kind of pixelated blur and, in a jumbled, pixelated blurry voice, I shout: "**If eat worm, bad polling nook!**"

Then I'm gone.

Other books by David Winship

Through The Wormhole, Literally, 2015, ISBN 978-1508718406

Stirring The Grass, 2016, ISBN 978-1492952725

Off The Frame, 2001, ISBN 978-1482793833

Talking Trousers and Other Stories, 2013, ISBN 978-1484898420